© Robert Ratliff 2017

Critical Point Marketing

For Digital Marketers

Critical Point Marketing

© Robert Ratliff 2017

Table of Contents

Chapter 1: What is Critical Point Marketing? 5

Chapter 2: Brief Description of Key Phrases 17

Chapter 3: Measuring Goals 23

Chapter 4: Search Engine Optimization 33

    The Trouble with SEO 35

    SEO Overview 37

    Location Information 39

    User Experience 40

    Social Media and SEO 40

    SEO Meta Tags (Hint- The Keyword Meta Tag is Unnecessary) 41

    Anchor Text for Hyperlinks 43

    Rich Snippets and Structured Data 44

    Site Content 45

SEO Summary 47

Chapter 5: The Power of PPC 49

    Setting Up Google PPC Ads 53

    Google Display Network Setup 61

    AdWords – Google PPC Summary 62

Chapter 6: Social Media Marketing 63

    Why Social Media Marketing? 63

    How to Use Social Media for Marketing 65

    Social Media Posts 65

    Paid Ads on Social Media 68

    Create Ads in Ads Manager 69

        Creating your campaign 69

        Choose your objective 69

        Name your campaign 70

        Creating your ad sets 70

Select your Page 70

Choose your audience 71

Select your ad placements 72

Set your budget and ad schedule 73

Set your bid 74

Naming your ad set 75

Creating your ads 75

Select an ad format 75

Choose your images 76

Add text to your ads 76

Social Media Summary 78

Chapter 7: Content Marketing 81

Food & Family Example 83

SEO & Content Marketing 83

Planning Your Content Marketing Campaign 84

Content Marketing Summary 85

Chapter 8: Video Marketing 87

Video Marketing PPV 92

Video Marketing Summary 94

Chapter 9: Email Marketing 95

Creating an Email List 97

Email Creation 99

Autoresponders 100

Chapter 10: Creating Landing Pages That Convert 103

Clear and Intriguing Headline 105

A Persuasive Subheadline 106

Good Quality Images 107

Who You Are and What You Do 108

A Clear and Concise Offer (What's in it for them.) 111

Testimonials 113

© Robert Ratliff 2017

Guarantee 113

Clear and Concise Call to Action 115

Setting up Future Sales Using Your landing Page 116

Landing Page Summary 117

Chapter 11: Measuring ROI 119

Tracking setup with Google Tag Manager 120

Tracking setup (web) 120

Tracking setup (app) 121

Creating a Facebook pixel for tracking 123

About the Facebook pixel code 124

Adding the Facebook pixel base code to your website's pages 127

Adding the event code to your website's pages 128

Install just the image tag of the Facebook pixel 131

Confirm your pixel is implemented correctly 133

Troubleshooting Pixel and Event Implementation 136

Troubleshooting Custom Conversions........................139

Troubleshooting Ad Performance...............................140

Defining conversions 142

Using custom events as conversions...........................142

Using a subset of standard events as conversions.......143

Running your campaign...144

Call Tracking...146

Call Tracking DNI..147

Measuring Results Summary 149

Chapter 12: Putting it all Together 151

© Robert Ratliff 2017

Critical Point Marketing

© Robert Ratliff 2017

Chapter 1: What is Critical Point Marketing?

Not too long ago, a man owned a gas station and was trying to figure out ways to increase his profits. One summer day while watching a man fill up his car, it occurred to him that the man had a wallet and in his wallet were dollars that he would spend if given the chance.

The owner of the gas station purchased a refrigerator and filled the refrigerator with bottles of soda and other drinks. He placed a small sign on the gas pumps informing them that there were cold drinks available for purchase inside. Of course many of his customers took advantage of this and the gas station owner began to see more and more possibilities.

The owner of the gas station then purchased food items and candy he could sell. Then bait and tackle. Then hunting equipment and so forth and so on until he had many people coming to his gas station for all types of things and his profits increased dramatically.

The point of this story is that there were critical points in which the owner of the gas station found an opportunity to increase profits and advertise other items. There was a

Critical Point Marketing

critical point where the customer was standing in front of the pump with dollars in his pocket. Once inside the small gas station store there was another critical point for marketing where the customer is standing at the counter ready to purchase his cold drink. That critical point was the perfect time to ask if the customer of he would like a sandwich with his drink or perhaps some candy. Another opportunity for marketing is the silent but sometimes effective placement of an item, like a package of M&Ms near the counter. You've seen this at your local grocery store or gas station as well.

There are critical points in which a potential customer or business should be engaged and targeted to produce the desired results of a marketing campaign. This first story illustrated critical marketing points in a NON-Digital example, here is an example in the digital world.

There is marketing and advertising going on all around us all the time. You hear ads on the radio, you see TV commercials, billboards, ads in the paper, on grocery carts, on cars, and online. Pretty much wherever you are, you are being advertised to in this day and age. However, this book is not about all forms of advertising, only the critical moments are the moments that count. These moments that give you the best chance to sell your products or services.

In the digital world there are these same critical points. Here's another example; A potential customer has noticed stains in her carpet. She is looking for a way to remove the stains. She takes her smartphone out and opens her mobile internet browser. Then searches Google for "how to remove carpet stains". This is a critical moment.

She sees an advertisement at the top of the screen that reads "how to remove carpet stains" she clicks the ad and is taken to an article a local carpet cleaning company has placed on their site. This is another critical moment.

At the top of this page there is an offer for "Carpet Cleaning and Stain Removal-3 Rooms only $149". The potential customer sees the offer, but decides not to act on the offer just yet. She wants to read the article first to determine if she can remove the stain herself.

She reads the article and finds very helpful information about stain removal, so much in fact that she decides she can do this herself. Following the instructions she tests to see if the stain is oil based or water based. It is oil based. She continues to follow the instructions until the stain is removed; mission accomplished. As she stands up she realizes that the area around the stain is much cleaner than the rest of the carpet, and that's when she realizes, she needs to have her carpets cleaned.

Pressed for time, she heads out the door to pick up her children from school putting the carpet cleaning thoughts behind her for a time.

Later that night she is browsing her Facebook feed when she sees a post showing the same special she saw on the website earlier that day. "Carpet Cleaning and Stain Removal-3 Rooms only $149". How convenient she thinks to herself. She puts the phone away for the night.

The next day she wakes up, walks into her office with a warm cup of coffee in hand, boots up her laptop and visits her favorite morning news site. There again she sees an ad for the same advertisement "Carpet Cleaning and Stain Removal-3 Rooms only $149". This time, she clicks on the ad to view more about the special offer. She is taken to a page which first and foremost shows the offer and the phone number to call. The fact that the offer was listed so many places legitimizes it.

Below the offer on this "Offer Page" she sees a short video showing the carpet cleaning process. The page identifies the strengths of the process like the deep clean, before and after photos and more. To strengthen the case for this special and the carpet cleaner, there are three testimonials indicating the amazing results and high quality customer service. Then again right after the testimonials, the phone number to call is displayed.

Knowing she has put this off far too long and knowing she needs to get her carpets cleaned, she picks up the phone and calls the business. After a four minute conversation, she has booked an appointment with the carpet cleaner and can now rest easier knowing that in two days' time her carpets will look like new again.

In this example as in most cases like this, there are several opportunities to connect with a potential customer. All of these potential points are critical points. This example also demonstrates the fact that in most cases, a single ad or single connection with a potential client is never enough. The business may need to connect with a potential customer four or five times before the customer will do business with you. The most important time to connect with a potential customer though is when that customer realizes they need your services.

In this book, we will be focusing on Digital Marketing and how to use various online tools from social media to Google. These tools with help you to better understand how to identify critical points in any marketing campaign where the potential customers must be engaged, and in what manor, in order to achieve the best return on your advertising investment.

Critical Point Marketing Numbers to Consider

There are many critical points in the sales process where digital marketing can be very effective. One of the most critical points is point when a potential customer is actively looking for your product or service. As you are probably aware, most people these days will start by researching a company or product via the internet. In fact, here are some recent polling numbers gleaned from several different sites regarding the latest internet research numbers from 2016:

1. 81% of Shoppers Conduct Online Research Before Buying
2. 88% of Consumers Trust Online Reviews as Much as a Personal Recommendation
3. 23% of Online Shoppers Fall Between The Ages of 35 and 44
4. 54% of Millennials Shop Online
5. Nearly 70% of Americans Shop Online
6. 55% of Shoppers Use Digital Coupons
7. Positive Reviews are More Important to Consumers Than Price

With these numbers in mind, you can see it's important to be found online when a potential customer is looking for a product or service you offer. There are several ways to achieve this and we will be focusing mainly on PPC, SEO, social media, and video.

Google's AdWords platform allows business owners to create advertisements that can be shared either on the search results page that is displayed when someone searches for your product or service or on a network of Google Authorized websites. The more critical of these two would be the search results page. The reason this page is so critical for better digital marketing is due to the fact that when people are searching for a product or service they are usually very close to making a buying decision or just starting their research. Either way, if you can get your business information in front of those potential customers you have an advantage over your competitors.

Most of the time when potential customers are looking for a product or service, they have already decided they want that product or service. When a potential client is looking for a new car, they will search online for something like "best cars of 2016" or "buy a new car". If the customer is looking for home service like a carpet cleaning professional, they are likely to search for something like "professional carpet cleaner" or "carpet cleaning companies".

A long time ago a cigarette company was in big trouble. They had taken months and gone through a few million dollars in order to rebrand their cigarette box. Unfortunately, they had decided to use the color green on their cigarette packaging. The problem was no one was wearing green and women would not purchase a packet of cigarettes that did not match their attire. What to do?

The cigarette company approached a man name PT Barnum. Mr. Barnum was a master of marketing and they needed help. Mr. Barnum they said, it will cost us as a company much too much to rebrand our cigarette packages to match the modern colors. PT Barnum had an idea.

Using a much smaller budget PT Barnum sent invitations to the most prestigious clothing designers in the world for a dinner to take place in NYC. He paid for their tickets, their hotel rooms, and of course their dinner. With the opportunity for the top designers to meet and get a free dinner, this was an offer too good to pass up and many if not all who were invited attended the event.

When they arrived they could see the room decorated in green, the dinner plates and napkins were green, and the table clothes were green. This, was a celebration of green. As dinner commenced top models of the day walked the stage in their new green apparel. After guest speakers talked about the good that green can do in the world it was settled, GREEN WAS THE NEXT BIG THING!

The following year the top clothing companies in the world started designing and producing green colored clothing and the little green package of cigarettes sold like gangbusters.

The moral of this story is that often times an idea can start something that can change an industry. It's in these critical moments and even before the idea is formed that a marketing campaign can begin to take effect. Marketing is all about planting ideas that will hopefully lead someday to an increase in revenue.

Here are a few examples of ideas planted by top companies:

- Drinking Coca Cola brings happiness
- Burger King insists that flame broiled tastes better
- BMW offers cars for those who have a passion for drive
- Without Cascade dishwashing detergent, your dishes will have spots, and spots are bad

There are many more examples, but planting ideas can have a powerful effect on sales and revenue. You don't always need to wait for a potential customer to need a carpet cleaner or to want your product before you advertise to them. Sometimes planting these ideas can create the need the customer didn't realize they had.

Because of this, there are some very critical points where being in the right place at the right time can make all the difference when it comes to converting leads to sales. As we look into many of the online tools available for marketing, my goal is to help you have a better understanding of each tool's use and how you can benefit from each tool. More importantly though, I want you to see how you can use the various online marketing tools in a synergetic manner for your marketing campaign to have more power and to be more effective than using each tool alone.

Keep in mind, that these chapters are only designed to give you a general overview of each subject not an in depth granular look. I want you to have a better understanding of each digital marketing tool covered here without spending too much time on specifics. So let's get started.

The tools we will be covering in the next few chapters are:

Critical Point Marketing

- SEO
- PPC
- Social Media
- Content Marketing
- Video Marketing
- Email Marketing
- Landing Pages

Chapter 2: Brief Description of Key Phrases

Before we go too much further, I'll take a moment to identify some of the key terms you will encounter as you read through this book.

Digital Marketing

Digital marketing is the process by which you engage your customers or potential customers digitally whether it be with online advertisements or digital content. These types of digital content can vary from podcasts and video to online articles and advertisements. For the most part, any type of content that is not in print or heard on the radio is going to be digital content.

SEO (Search Engine Optimization)

SEO is the process by which your digital content is optimized in a way that Google will recognize the content as being the highest quality and most relevant content associated with an online search. This process of optimizing your content doesn't take long, however, it may take months before Google will see the whole of your content as being front page worthy. In some cases, however, certain articles and videos can rank quickly, sometimes within just a few hours. We will discuss this in greater detail in Chapter 5.

Social Media

Social media for many people means one thing: "Facebook". Social media can take several different forms pertaining to anything that engages a person online socially. These social sites can include dating sites, image sharing sites, online forums, and more.

PPC (Pay-per-click)

PPC to most people means money you spend with Google for ads on the Google search results page. PPC does come in many forms though. There are many places online you can pay-per-click. In general, pay-per-click means that each time someone clicks on your ad, you will be billed. The amount you will be billed varies. Places you can place ads are all around the internet, from news sites, to social media and dating sites. You may be surprised at all the places you can place an ad and pay-per-click.

CPC (Cost-per-click)

Cost-per-click is the amount of money you spend for each click. Cost-per-click is usually shown as an average. If one click costs you $3 and another click costs you $1, then the average cost-per-click for those two clicks is then $2.

Impressions

Impressions is the term used to describe the number of times your ad is seen. Your ad may be shown to 100 people but you may find only 2 people who saw your ad clicked on your ad. Ad impressions take place anytime your ad is shown online whether it's as an ad on the Google search results page, or an ad placed on Facebook, dating sites, other websites, or your own site.

Click Through Rate

Click through rate is a number derived by taking the number of clicks your ad receives divided by the number of ad impressions. If your ad is seen 100 times and your ad is clicked 3 times, then your click through rate is 3/100 or 3%. Click through rates can be influenced by multiple factors.

PPV (Pay-per-view)

PPV is essentially the same as pay-per-click. The difference is that with PPV you are paying for each viewing. For example for a YouTube video with PPV, you would pay every time your video was played.

Google Search Network

The Google Search Network allows you to place an ad on the search results page. The search results page is the page that lists all of the results Google can find relevant to the search that others performed. You'll see Google Search Network ads at the top and the bottom of the search results page.

Google Display Network

Google Display Network ads are the ads that you see on other websites. Sometimes these ads are images, sometimes these ads appear as words similar to search network ads. The display network allows you to place ads on many different sites from news sites to niche blog sites. The Google Display Network also allows for retargeting and remarketing.

Retargeting and Remarketing

These words are usually interchangeable. Retargeting and remarketing means when someone visits your website we can place a "cookie" (a small code snippet) on a user's browser. Once this cookie is placed, both Google and Facebook can now show your ads to anyone who has visited your website for up to 30 days or until the user clears / deletes their cookies.

You've seen this techniques used when you have visited a shopping site like Amazon and then notice that the product you were looking at previously seems to follow you around the web tempting you over and over to make the purchase.

Landing Page

A landing page is a page users "land on" when they click on your ad or click on a link in an article or search engine. It's possible that any and every page on your website could potentially be a landing page. For advertising purposes especially, a custom built landing page created for the specific purpose of converting a page visit to a sale or booking can be the difference between success and failure of your marketing campaign. The page that users land on is usually the first impression they receive about your service or product. Good landing pages are vital for digital marketing success. You will learn more about creating high quality landing pages in a later chapter.

Chapter 3: Measuring Goals

The goal of most marketing is to engage the customer in order to create leads, share a message and more. For any marketing campaign, the first step in creating the campaign is to set an end goal. In other words before the results of a marketing campaign *can* be measured, we must first identify how the particular marketing results *should* be measured. Below is a list of a few results that a marketing campaign may be designed to affect.

1. Create Sales Leads
2. Increase Brand Awareness
3. Increase Product Awareness
4. Increase Positive Perception in a Company - Locally or Globally
5. Increase Market Share
6. Increase Sales/Profits
7. Increase Newsletter Subscriptions – Email List

Let it be said too that the list above can be further sub-categorized into a much more granular list of measurements.

In this book, you will be introduced to concepts that will help you identify the critical points where your marketing campaign must touch the potential customer or group of potential customers in a particular way in an order to increase the possible return on investment of your marketing campaign.

Let's take a quick moment to address some of these goals and how we may measure them. As we take moment consider how to measure these goals let's again look at the various ways we can move the needle in each category.

Sales Leads

Sales leads come in many different forms. In the most obvious sense, a sales lead can be in the form of a phone number or email address of someone requesting more information about a product or services you offer. These types of leads are direct leads. "I want information about your product or service, therefore I am giving you my contact information or calling you".

There are indirect types of sales leads too. These leads may be a potential customer who is interested in learning more about the field in which you operate. "I am not right now looking for a carpet cleaner, but I am looking at how to remove a stain". You read about how this may happen in the first chapter. An indirect lead can also be a person who started following you on Facebook but may not do business with you for up to a year or more.

When you are looking to track these leads, both direct and indirect, you will find you are going to track everything from the number of email addresses you receive to the number of phone calls you take and even the number of people following you on your social media sites. Anytime you have created an opportunity to reach out to your prospective customers whether it be through social channels or emails and phone calls, you've created a potential sale and there for a lead.

Increase Brand Awareness

To measure your company's brand awareness, or "mindshare" (marketing jargon for brand awareness), again, you will find there are many ways. The best way to measure mindshare is to perform a survey in your area. This survey can be performed via outbound phone calls to locals in your community or can be performed standing on the streets in a populated area. A simple one question survey can be all you need. The question: "Have you heard of ABC Company?" If one person for every 100 surveyed have heard of your company you have a 1% mindshare. You get the point.

In the digital world there are some other measurements that can help you at least know what reach you potentially may have achieved. Usually these metrics are measured by the number of impressions your ads have received. If you are running a Facebook ad in your community and targeting only those in your community, then you can at least tell by the ad impressions how many people in your community potentially were able to see your ad. If you have 60,000 people in your community ad your ad impressions show your ad has been seen by 6000 people, then you know at least in some part that around 10% of the people in your targeted area saw your ad. Again, however, this will only give you a partial idea. There is no way to guarantee that all 6000 people who saw your ad will remember the name of your company or know what you do.

Increase Product Awareness

There is not a sure way to tell if people have heard of your product or service unless you ask. As mentioned above though, you can measure the number of people who have potentially seen an advertisement about your product or service by looking at the number of ad impressions your data shows. Remember though just because they saw your ad, that doesn't mean they'll remember your product or what it does.

Increase Positive Perception in a Company - Locally or Globally

In the field of marketing, the perception of your company is sometimes referred to as "Heart Share". Heart share is the next measurement after mindshare. With an increase in mindshare, you know more people have heard of you or your product. The next question is "how do you feel about, or what do you think about the product, service, or company in general?"

In this digital age, a common measurement of perception is online reviews. Is your company's customer review status two stars, three stars, or five stars? It's very important to pay close attention to these reviews. Often negative reviews can be beneficial, because they point out the pros and cons in your customer service, product, or fulfilment system.

Customer satisfaction surveys can also help you to better understand how your current or past customers feel about your product or service. An important question to be asking yourself is: how do those who have never used your product or service feel about it. Again a survey will deliver the best and most quantitative results. The choice is do you conduct a survey online, or over the phone or both? Both an online and offline survey will give you the broadest measurement.

Increase Market Share

Market share measures how much of the market your product or service controls. There are many ways to measure market share. One of the most general ways to measure market share is to take the number of products or services you have sold to individuals in your market and divide it by the total number of potential customers.

If you are a local service provider like a carpet cleaner, then you would take the total number of people and businesses in your area and divide that by the number of customers you have cleaned carpets for over the past couple of years. You can measure that rate over the last year if you want to be more aggressive. While there are other considerations to make like the number of homes and business that have carpets, measuring the market shared with the general population can at least give you a starting point.

In this example let's say you service an area that has a population of 100,000 people and you have cleaned the carpets for 1,000 separate individuals over the past year. Your market share will then be 1%. If you would like to be more specific, you can narrow the 100,000 people to an estimated 50,000 people who have carpets to clean and who are old enough to hire a carpet cleaner. If you have cleaned the carpets for the same 1,000 different individuals, then it's safe to say you have about a 2% market share in your area.

As you look to measure your increase in market share, in the above example, by gaining an additional 100 clients whom you've never cleaned carpets for, while maintaining the 1,000 clients you had, you can then estimate a 10% increase in market share.

Increase Sales & Profits

This is another fairly easy statistic to measure. The easiest way to measure your increase in sales is to look at the amount of revenue generated this year vs last year. If you made $200,000 gross revenue last year with a net profit of $80,000 and this year you made a gross profit of $220,000 and a net profit of $88,000 then you have made an increase of roughly 10% in both areas.

You may also want to measure things like the number of jobs sold, or the number of products sold year over year. The bottom line is if you are spending advertising dollars then you want to see a healthy and positive return on that investment. Measuring sales and profitability is a great way to tell if your marketing is effective or if you need to change your tactic.

Remember though, sometimes when you have a long term growth strategy in place an immediate jump in numbers may not be the most important measurement. You may also look at an increase in newsletter subscribers and Facebook followers as a big step toward better profits in the long term.

Increase Newsletter Subscriptions – Email Lists

A good marketing plan may not always be supported by sales and profits alone. In many cases people who subscribe to a newsletter may not become a customer for a year or more. The secret though is that once you are able to add a potential customer to your database you gain a better chance at winning their business over time. In other words, a newsletter subscription today could mean money earned on next year's books.

Marketing Growth

No matter what your goals are when it comes to executing a marketing campaign, one of the keys to a successful campaign is to understand what you are trying to increase. A successful marketing campaign can mean increasing brand awareness, adding to your customer database or increase sales and profitability. If you don't know what you are trying to achieve during your campaign you are automatically setting yourself up for failure. The better you understand what your goals of your marketing campaign are, the more successful it will be.

In the next chapter, we will start looking at how each of the digital marketing tools discussed thus far can be used to create and execute a good marketing strategy and how to get the most out of your marketing campaign.

Let's start by taking a look at how an idea can be turned into profits....

Chapter 4: Search Engine Optimization

Let's start with the basics of SEO. What is it and why it matters. SEO is an art. It is the art of organizing a website in such a way that Google will give you better search rankings so that when a potential customers searches for your type of product or service in an area you service they will find you. So the question is do you want to come up on the first page in the search results?

Your answer should undoubtedly be "YES"!

If the answer is yes, then that means you want your site to be optimized for search results. Mostly Google. Now I know there are other search engines out there like Bing, but here is the issue: Independent studies show that around 90% of the population uses Google when they do searches online and the other search engines combined only account for around 10% of the searches. So where do we put our focus? Google. The other search engines will usually fall in line, meaning if you have good search results in Google, then you will most likely have good results in Bing, Yahoo, and others.

Maybe you've heard something like SEO is dead and Google

is making it harder and harder to optimize your website. The answer is yes they are. You see, every time someone finds a way to somehow "game the rankings", they will share it with a friend, then that friend shares it with another friend and so forth and so on until everyone is optimizing their sites using that tactic.

When Google catches that, they then find a way to fix the programing so that these strategies won't work. For example, back in the day, you could add keywords that you want to be ranked for by the hundreds in the bottom of your website, perhaps in a white font on a white background, and guess what, now your site has more of that keyword than anyone else, so now you get top page rankings. Well, Google caught onto that, and now if you have too many of the same search phrases on a page, it can actually hurt you rather than help you. So, Google is doing their best to isolate poor SEO tactics and keep people from cheating.

Google, however, does tell us what we need to do in order to rank well, and even wrote a short document about it. Long story short, Google says if you want to be ranked well on the first page, then make it easy for the user to find the information they are looking for in a way that keeps their attention and is interesting enough that they want more information. So that is what we work on, making it easier for the user to find the information and make it interesting and engaging.

The Trouble with SEO

Here's the rub. One, first page rankings don't always mean sales, or jobs. Even when your site is on the first page of results, you share that link with 20 or so other business who are all trying to get business in your area for the same services you offer.

Two, many times, people won't even SEARCH the web for a service if they have used the service before, or if they are sent an offer that gets their attention before they need to search. For example: When you get hungry for a burger, do you run to Google, type in "burger" and see where to get your lunch. Not always. You usually just go to places you have already been.

A lot of digital marketing lies around branding and advertising to drive traffic to your website. A good coupon in the mail, or a well targeted ad on Facebook can get your attention. That's one of the reasons that social media marketing can be effective in helping attract new customers. We will cover more on social media marketing later in this book.

Here's the deal. Most people feel that if they sign up for SEO services to optimize their site, they are going to start immediately getting leads because of the SEO efforts. While SEO is important and you do need to be ranking high in search results, it's also only one of the pieces in this very large Digital Marketing Puzzle and SEO does not generate leads. SEO simply gets you ranking on the first page of Google, Yahoo, Bing, and more. Lead generation is accomplished by driving traffic to your site, giving the customer offers to choose from, having testimonials and satisfaction guarantees on your site so the customer has a reason to pick up the phone and call you.

SEO can help people find you, but when a client relies only on SEO for lead generation, they are usually disappointed. The bottom line is you need to be more attractive in your community and potential customers need to know who you are and want to click on your link, and if they don't, then you're just another link among twenty links, even if you are on the first page of the search results.

In summary, SEO is important in order to help you show up on the first page of the search results, but your branding, social sharing, and ad placement in various areas in the online world are just as important. Potential customers need to find you, but they also need to like you, your service, and your solutions to their problems, before you are going to generate a sale. Now that we've covered how SEO plays a role in your digital marketing, let's learn about how to optimize a website and why.

SEO Overview

The reason we optimize a website for search engines is to ensure search engines can find the information they need from your website to best understand your website. Google will upload all the information about your website into their servers, where it will have access to the website's information and code. Google doesn't crawl the internet every time you do a search. In reality Google searches its own database each time. Google then applies an algorithm during each search assigning points, for lack of a better word, to the various data it has collected about your site. No one but Google has access to that algorithm and very few know what the algorithm contains. It is kept secret.

What we do know is that optimizing a site these days takes a lot more than just adding keywords and description tags to your pages. Google is rewriting its algorithms every day to focus on its user's experience.

When a customer is looking for carpet cleaning, Google knows the user is most likely looking for help cleaning their carpets from a local professional. For this reason, Google is going to look through its database for a website that has information about carpet cleaning in the potential customer's area. Google will look for pages that show information about carpet cleaning, what tools are used, how effective your carpet cleaning may be, what the costs for this services will most likely be, what kind of specials are available and how other people feel about the services. For this reason, a carpet cleaning page must contain some if not all of these answers.

Below is a list showing the types of data a potential customer may want and how Google may look to determine the best fit for the search.

1. Is the carpet cleaning local:>>>Lookup the business address or relevant location information
2. What will it cost :>>> Look for a site that explains costs associated with carpet cleaning in my area.
3. What cleaning process does this carpet company use and how effective is it :>>> is there information on this page about the carpet cleaning process and solutions used?
4. How do others feel about the service :>>> Find testimonials from people in my area
5. Do people find the site content helpful :>>> How many pages do users view and how long are do they stay on the website?

Location Information

When it comes to location information about your business, Google not only wants to see what address you have listed on your web page is, but will also look to see if your company's address is consistent on other websites. Google will check your Google Business Page, but will also look for your address information on sites like government sites, business directory and licensing sites, the local chamber of commerce, and more. Google does have the ability to verify your address by photo that either they take with their street camera, or that you upload to your Google business page.

User Experience

Google is also looking for the sites that are easier to navigate and are mobile friendly. These days more than 60% of all web traffic is accessed via mobile devices. Therefore, if your website is not mobile friendly, Google will rank your site lower. This is especially true if a user is performing their search on a mobile device.

Social Media and SEO

Another trick Google has up its sleeve is that it will gage how good your information is based on how many shares your site has in the social media arena. Google monitors sites like Twitter, Facebook, and other social media sites to see if others are talking about or sharing the information on your website. If people are sharing your site, then the information must be interesting. At least that's how Google sees it.

SEO Meta Tags (Hint- The Keyword Meta Tag is Unnecessary)

In order to effectively Search Engine Optimize a website, you are going to want to make sure that your site is easy to navigate and make sure visitors can find the information they are looking for easily. You will want to add good page titles and title tags. Title tags are the tags that look like this in your page code:

<title>Business Cards </title>

This tag should summarize the content on the page effectively. You will want to make sure the content is relevant to the search you're hoping to be ranked for. You may want to add bullet points to make it easier to see the main points you're trying to portray on your pages. You can also highlight or bold words that are important for your visitors to know.

Next you will want to make sure you have a good page

description in your description tag. Your description tag, again is a meta tag found in your code that

Using "heading tags" appropriately can help too. Heading tags are those tags in your website code that look like this: <H1>. There are various levels of heading tags much like an outline. Google seems to add particular value to the <H1> tag, but if you have too many on a single page then the points you get are diluted. In order to use headings effectively, you will want to use the heading tags like this:

<h1>Business Cards</h2>

<h2> High Gloss Business Cards</h2>

Information about business cards goes here.

<h3>Black High Gloss Business Cards</h3>

Information about black high gloss business cards goes here.

<h3>White High Gloss Business Cards</h3>

Information about white high gloss business cards goes here.

The main heading tag, (<H1>), should be the main subject of

the page content. All other heading tags should use <h2>,<h3>,<h4>, etc. Again these heading tags will act much like an outline. You will want to stay away from using multiple <H1> tags on a single page. It would be better, if you have a new subject requiring an overall <H1>heading, to create a new page that introduces the new subject. You will then want to link to that page from a main menu, or you may even want to link to that new page from the page you just created if the new heading is related to the previous page.

Anchor Text for Hyperlinks

In the above example, we used an SEO tactic that makes it easier for the user to know where a link will take them. This is known as anchor text. An anchor text is hypertext that is linked to another web page. In this example, the anchor text for the two links is "high gloss business cards" and "flat, no gloss business cards". Each link is underlined making it easy for the user to find and letting them know the text is most likely a link to another page. Anchor text is a great way to link from one page to another and lets the user know what to expect once they click on the link Google tells us that we want to make sure the links are easy to find and stand out on a page.

Rich Snippets and Structured Data

As Google indicates,

> "when you use structured data to markup content, you help Google better understand its context for display in Search, and you achieve better distribution of your content to users from Search. You do this by marking up content properties and enabling actions where relevant. This makes it eligible for inclusion in Rich Cards and Rich Snippets. For some content types, it allows users to engage directly with your content right from Search. This markup is also the first step to making some content eligible for lists and host-specific list previews. See Mark Up Your Lists for more details".

Rich snippets and other structured data can help Google better understand your website which can lead to better SEO. There is no secret silver bullet you can use to dominate the Google.

There are too many parameters that Google uses to rank a website. Everything you do can help a little, but there is not one thing that will make the difference to guarantee you first page presence other than paying to be on the first page using Google PPC campaigns.

Site Content

Of all the items Google uses to rank your site, one of the most valuable is the content of the website. Good content on a website leads to better rankings for several reasons. Most importantly, the content of each website contains information Google can crawl on a regular basis in order to determine what content the searcher may be looking for. Good content is unique and filled with quality information the end user will also find helpful.

In order to determine if your content is high quality content, Google measures the amount of time a visitor spends on the site and the number of pages a visitor views. If your content is truly unique and helpful then it makes sense that a site visitor will stay longer to learn more about your product or service. These two metrics are called bounce rate and session time.

Bounce rate. According to Google,

> "Bounce Rate is the percentage of single-page sessions (i.e. sessions in which the person left your site from the entrance page without interacting with the page)." In other words, if you have 100 visitors and 80 left without viewing more than one page, your bounce rate is 80% - 80/100. If you have a high percentage of visitors who leave your website without looking at more than one page, it's possible your content is not engaging or interesting.
>
> Session time. Session time is also a key indicator of quality content. If a visitor to your website spends a high amount of time on your website, then that is a key indicator that your site's content is good quality, meaning it's engaging and interesting. High session times also indicate that the content

on your site is the type of content the visitor is looking for when they performed the search that lead to your site. "

SEO Summary

SEO is much, much more than a matter of adding key search terms into your Meta tags and content. Sites that are ranked higher are ranked higher because their content is engaging, unique, interesting and gives the visitor the information they are looking for. High ranking sites are also some of the easiest to navigate.

As mentioned earlier, SEO alone is not the answer to increased revenue and lead generation. PPC advertising is another tool that you can use alongside SEO to help your business. Now let's take a look into the power of pay-per-click advertising.

Critical Point Marketing

Chapter 5: The Power of PPC

The real power of Google's pay-per-click (PPC) program is that it allows anyone to advertise to potential customers the moment they are looking for those products or services. When you have a high quality ad that links to a high quality web page, and you meet the bid for a specific search term, you can virtually guarantee first page rankings. This is one of the most critical times to engage with a potential customer.

Critical point marketing means engaging potential customers at critical points in their buying process. One of the most valued engagements is introducing your product or services to a potential buyer the moment they start researching that product or service. In many cases, one of the first steps in becoming a customer, in the 21st century, is searching for information about that product or service on a search engine, like Google. If you can engage with the customer at the exact moment they are looking for your product or service, you have a huge advantage over your competitor.

Google's AdWords is the supplementary program that supports their PPC system. The AdWords program offers two basic networks for running ads, the "Search Network" and the "Display Network".

According to Google the search network is: "A group of search-related websites where your ads can appear.

- Websites include Google search sites, as well as other Google sites and non-Google websites that partner with Google to show ads (search partners).
- When you advertise on the Search Network, your ad can show next to search results when someone searches with terms related to one of your keywords.
- The Search Network is part of the Google Network, our name for all the webpages and apps where AdWords ads can appear."

Again, according to Google, "The Google Display Network allows to you connect with customers with a variety of ad formats across the digital universe. This network spans over two million websites that reach over 90% of people on the Internet. It can help you reach people while they're browsing their favorite websites, showing a friend a YouTube video, checking their Gmail account, or using mobile sites and apps."

Display network ads can and in most cases should be image ads. Google has a tool ready in their ad management system that will help you create image ads. Image ads should contain a good quality image that is eye catching and interesting, and having your phone number listed on the ad itself can help promote calls.

The best way to distinguish the difference is to understand that the search network shows your ads to potential customers when they are actively searching for your product or service. The display network is a network of websites where potential customers can see your company's ads whether they are searching for them or not. On the display network, your ads will appear as images or text on other websites that may or may not be relative to the content your website offers.

The display network, much like the aisle at your local grocery store, it gives you an opportunity to place ads in front of potential client who may not be searching for your product or service. It is possible, however, to select a certain type of demographic to target on the display network. Rather than casting your pearls before swine, it is possible to show your ads to customers who aren't actively searching for your company, but who may have an interest in your products or services later down the road.

The display network also allows you to target customers who have recently visited your website. This form of advertising is call retargeting. Retargeting means when a customer visits your website, a small snippet of code can be dropped into their web browser called a "cookie". Once the cookie has been placed anytime it's allowed, the visitor to your website will now see your ad on any site that allows Google display network ads to be shown. You've seen retargeting in action when you have looked for a product on Amazon and then see that product over and over on every site you visit it seems.

The beauty of retargeting is that once someone has visited your website they will continue to see an ad for your products and services. It will increase their mindshare and help them to remember you when they do decide to purchase a product or service you offer. Retargeting in some ways can also make your business seem larger and more engaged in the community since potential customer will now see your ad everywhere they go online for the next month or so.

Another advantage of using Google's display network is that when a potential customer clicks on a display network ad you create, the cost per click is significantly lower than it would be on the search network. The disadvantage to display network ads is that the potential customer may or may not be actively looking to purchase the products or services you offer at that moment. This means you may pay for clicks on your ad, but may not see an income generated from that click for several weeks or months.

Setting Up Google PPC Ads

To sign up for the Google AdWords pay-per-click program, visit adwords.google.com. There will be several questions to answer and a step by step walkthrough to help you get started. If you missed this walkthrough or had to put it off for a time, here are the basic steps.

1. First you will be asked to set up your campaign. You will need to select the type of campaign you are running. The campaign types are "search network" and the aforementioned "display network", or "search partner" network.

2. Next you will want to choose the geographic location

where you'd like your ads to show. You can choose your target locations by zip code, city name, or with latitude longitude coordinates. Search for the most appropriate area for your business.

3. You will also have the opportunity to select a type of bid strategy and set a daily budget. By selecting the manual bid strategy, you will have more control. If you decide to set an automatic bid strategy then Google will determine the best cost per click for your campaign. If you do choose to let Google set the bids, I would place max cost per click you are willing to pay. I've seen up to 50% savings on clicks just by setting a lower cost per click. The downside is, you may not have top of the page ads all the time, but when you are just starting, it may be worth it until you get more of an income to offset your marketing costs. Remember, you can always change these settings later once you understand how to use the AdWords program a little better.

Setting a daily budget sets the maximum that Google is authorized to charge you per day. Although there isn't a way to set a weekly or monthly budget, choosing a daily budget will help you set the weekly and monthly budgets. For example, setting a daily budget of $30 per day is setting a budget of $210 per week. Or $30 X 7. Charges for your clicks will be billed in increments of $50 when you start. If you take 10 days to reach $50 then your total spend for the month would be around $150.

Setting a daily budget is important so if you do end up making a mistake or if your ads aren't converting to sales, you can prevent big losses until you fix the problem. Once you have determined that your advertising dollars are converting to sales then you can bump up the daily budget.

One thought process when it comes to an advertising budget, especially pay-per-click, is to spend for desired results. In other words, if you know you are generating $4 for every $1 you spend, then you know if you want to earn $2,400 a month you need to spend $600 per month.

In one example, I once listened to a business talk about how they took home a $2 Million dollar profit, after spending $20 Million dollars in advertising to generate $22 Million in net revenue. The moral of the story is, if you have to spend $1 in order to make a net profit of $0.20, the campaign is still making money. Once you know you will be in the black, it's only a matter of determining how much you want to earn to determine how much you are willing to spend.

4. You can choose to ignore the "Ad Extensions" section for now. This is an important part of any campaign, but you can add these later after you've finished creating your campaign. If you do want to add ad extensions, you can do so by clicking the ad extensions tab in your campaign and add them.

Ad extensions are additional information snippets you can add to your ad, like phone numbers, up to four different web pages, a click to call button, location, directions, and more. These extensions can help you attract more buyers by making it easier for them to find and contact you.

5. When it's time to start creating the ad, you will first need to name your ad group. Once you've created and named your ad group, you should be guided through the process of creating your first ad. If for some reason you are not taken

through this process, in order to create an ad, you will click on the tab called "Ads". Once on that screen, you will see a button that reads "+Ad" you click that button to start creating a new ad.

Keep in mind that more people click on ads when the headline includes the keyword they're searching for. When you use your keywords in your headline it can help you gain a higher click through rate. You are going to be limited to 25 characters here, so you will want to make sure you use that space wisely. The headline should be related to the search keywords you want to be found for, and also enticing so potential clients will be more likely to click the ad.

The second and third lines allow for 35 characters of text each. In most markets, you'll be more successful if you describe a benefit on the second line, followed by a feature or offer on the third line. You may want to create a few ads with different headlines, and subheadlines to determine which ad type is getting a better click through rate.

Even though Google places the field for your display URL, which is the web address people see in your ad, below your main ad copy, it won't actually be there when your ad is live. When your ad displays on the search results page, its URL will instead show up right below your headline. The display URL has to have the same domain as your site, though the URL itself doesn't necessarily have to be the specific landing page that you take people to.

The last line is your actual destination URL, or specific chosen landing page. You can also use a tracking link here. Remember, your landing pages can also make the difference between a sale, booking or just another site visitor. Again, you can test different types of ads and landing pages to find the best combination for you. The better the combination the better your sales and bookings will be. This is a process called AB or Split testing.

Here are a few examples of an AdWords Search ad with various ad extensions.

Amherst Ice Cream Parlour
Ad www.example.com
(413) 123-4567
Our specialty is pistachio.
English majors, buy 1 get 1 free.
📍 100 Dardanelles Rd, Amherst MA

Mushroom Foraging Tours
`Ad` www.example.com
Find chanterelle, porcini, oyster mushrooms with a fungi guide!
"So impressed. Brought home a pound of ceps." - exampleblog.com

Acme Electronics
`Ad` www.example.com
Shop ACME Electronics for laptops, smartphones, video games and more!
Free shipping • 24-7 customer service • Price matching

6. Once you have created your ad, the next step is to decide which search phrases you want your ad to be found under. Once you reach this point you will either be walked through this process, or you will click on the "Keywords" tab to access the keywords and search phrases you want potential customers to use to see your ad. Paste in your keywords. Start with just one set, and add plus signs (+), brackets ([ ]), and quotes (" ") to see precisely how many searches of each type you'll get. When you're getting started, it's not a good idea to dump hundreds or thousands of keywords in. Start with a tiny handful of important ones, and work from there.

7. Again, you can edit or set your maximum cost per click (called your default bid), but know that every keyword is

theoretically a different market, which means that it is possible to set a maximum cost per click for each of your major keywords or search phrases.

If you can only afford $50 per day instead of, say, $170, it's better to bid on low-cost keywords so that your ad can be seen by as many people as possible during the day. Due to the limitations of any budget, if you're going after high-priced keywords, you may go through your entire budget in just a few hours and your ad will no longer be shown throughout the day. The daily budget will reset every 24 hours.

8. Now that you have created your ad, added in your budget, determined, and set your maximum cost per click, you will want to review everything. Double-check your ad, keyword, and search phrases. Check your cost per click to be sure you get the positions on the page you want. Remember to double check your daily budget. You don't want to max out your credit card or empty your bank account on day one.

9. The last step before your ads will run is to enter your billing and credit card or debit card information. Your ads will start running as soon as you confirm your payment

information. Be sure you check your ad campaigns daily to determine if you are getting clicks, and look for opportunities to test different ads to maximize your results.

Google Display Network Setup

Creating ads and ad campaigns using Google's display network is exactly the same. When you start to create your campaign, you can choose to use only the "search network" or you can choose to show your ads on the "search network" or "display network" if you don't create an image ad, the ad you created for the search network will be the same, but shown on the display network. Again, this means your ad will be shown on someone else's website rather than in the search results.

You can also create image ads for the display network by uploading images and a chosen text in the image ad creation tool in the Google AdWords platform. Search network ads are a great way to place an idea in a potential customer's mind who may not be looking, at least at the moment, for your product or service. Display network and image ads are a great way to get potential customers in a specific market interested in your product or service.

Search Network Ads also allow for retargeting. Again, this is a very powerful too.

AdWords – Google PPC Summary

Running ads through Google's search network is a great way and a critical point in which to reach your potential customers. PPC can virtually guarantee you first page rankings when potential customers search for your product or service. Making it easy for potential customers to learn more about your business at the moment they are looking for your type of business can cause a major boost in your income when managed correctly.

Chapter 6: Social Media Marketing

Social media marketing is an important part of any marketing campaign. Earlier in this book we talked about the different types of marketing components. These three components were Market Share, Mind Share, and Heart Share. Market share if you recall is all about how much of the market your business services and controls.

The top three social media sites are Instagram, Facebook, and Twitter. Posting on all three of these sites can help you increase your mind share and brand awareness. Each social media platform as different strengths. Of the three, Facebook tends to offer the best fit for marketing products and services. If you have the budget and time, advertising on all three would still be the best choice. Every little bit helps when trying to build a good marketing foundation online.

Why Social Media Marketing?

Mind share is all about bringing your business to the forefront of a potential customer's mind in your market. In other words, when you ask someone to name a carpet cleaner, who do they think of? If more people think about your business, then you have the best mind share in the area. If you ask around, and no one mentions your business, you have some work to do.

Heart share again is measured by determining how people generally feel about your business, do they like your business, and do they have good feelings about your business. Heart share can also be reflected in the reviews you receive. If you have a two of five star rating rather than a five of five star rating, again, you have some work to do.

Social media marketing is an excellent way to get information about your business in front of people in your community or service area. If you offer products worldwide, social media is still a great way to reach potential customers, you will just need a rather large budget in order to create worldwide mind share and heart share.

For a local business, Social Media can be very effective since you can target potential customers in the community you serve with a much smaller budget. Of course, it depends on the number of people you are trying to target. The more people you are trying to target, the more money you will need to allocate to social media marketing.

How to Use Social Media for Marketing

In the next few sections we will be discussing the different aspects of social media marketing from posting tweets to paid ads and targeting. You may want to keep in mind as we discuss these ideas what type of market you are in, who your customers are. Things to think about are:

- Where are your customers located?
- What is there income?
- Are they married?
- Do they have children?
- What are their interests?

The more you know about your target customers, the better you can advertise to them. Facebook allows you to target specific audiences based on these demographics and psychographics, plus a lot more. First let's talk about the purpose of posting on social media and how.

Social Media Posts

The concept of posting, when it comes to social media, is

more about keeping your business on the forefront of people's minds. If you really want to make sure that others remember you, you need to make sure that there is some kind of emotional attachment formed. When you think about the posts that you remember the most, you will most likely remember the posts that made you feel happy, sad, or even angry.

Social media marketing is key to raising awareness for your company in a given geographic area, because you can literally get your name, and your ideas right where many people spend a lot of their time. In fact, here is why advertising on Facebook is such a good idea:

- As of third quarter 2016 Facebook had 1.79 billion monthly active users.
- 1.57 billion of those users used a mobile device
- 55% of all Facebook users are men and 45% are women
- 87% of adults 18–29 use Facebook.
- 73% of adults 30–49 use Facebook.
- 63% of adults 50–64 use Facebook.
- 56% of adults 65+ use Facebook.

- 14% of the Facebook audience lives in the US (238 Million)

According to DailyMail.co.uk, around 70% of smartphone users are frequent Facebook visitors, with more than half of them checking it every day. Peak Facebook time is during the evening, just before bed. On average, we visit the Facebook app or the site **13.8** times during the day, for two minutes and **22** seconds each time. This means the average amount of time a person spends on Facebook is around 30 minute each day.

In the past, before the digital world, advertising was limited to print materials, or radio and television. Print materials were sometimes saved, but many times, the printed ads end up in the garbage. Radio and television ads are great when it comes to reaching a large audience. The downside is once these types of ads finish running, they are easily forgotten. These legacy types of advertising are also very expensive in many cases.

The power of social media is that it allows a business to make themselves known to individuals daily, help form an emotional connection, and the post will stay on the potential customers Facebook feed. Social media ads and posts are also still very inexpensive when compared to legacy marketing mediums, but you still get targeted trackable results.

Because of the need to build an emotional connection with your audience in order to improve brand awareness, you do not want your posts to be a stream of offers and specials. If all you're doing with your posts is trying to sell your audience something, you will find you lose followers. One of the rules of digital marketing is the 4-1-1 rule. That rule states that you post 4 interesting, funny, or other type of emotional posts, 1 offer, and 1 soft offer. A soft offer could be an invitation like your page or join your newsletter, but is not asking for the follower to purchase anything. Keep your posts engaging. You don't need to sell something every time you post.

Paid Ads on Social Media

Facebook and Instagram allow you to post ads and offers or boost posts to thousands of people from one platform, the Facebook Ads Manager. Twitter campaigns are a little different. To create ads through Twitter you will login to their ads manager found at ads.twitter.com and log in there. In this chapter we aren't going to go through the steps to create a Twitter campaign, but you will find the setup is very similar to a Facebook campaign which we are going to show here.

Facebook has a very simple step by step system, that they will take you through, when you are ready to place an ad. You will find the process is very similar to the Google PPC campaign setup. You will first select your audience and budget and then create your ad.

Here is the process for creating a Facebook ad:

Create Ads in Ads Manager

To create an ad campaign in Facebook's ad creation tool, go to Ads Manager and click **Create Campaign**. Ad Creation takes you through the process of:

Creating your campaign

Choose your objective

The first step in creating an ad in ad creation is choosing an objective from the list.

Critical Point Marketing

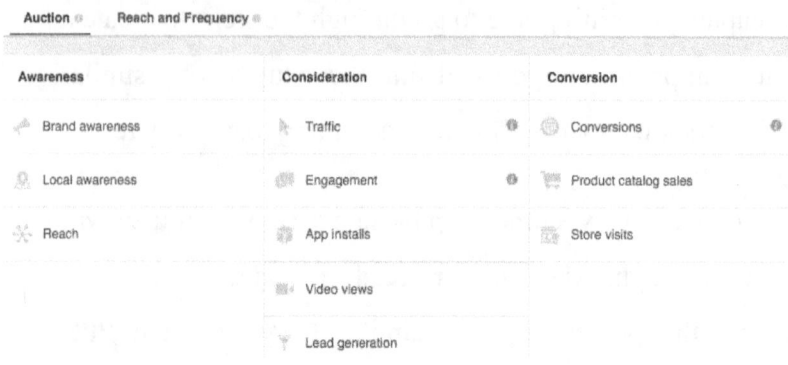

Name your campaign

Next to **Campaign Name**, add a name for your campaign or use the default name that appears.

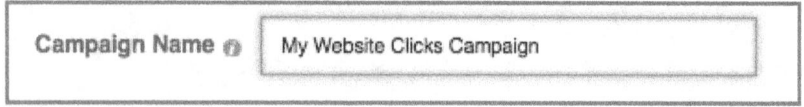

Creating your ad sets

Select your Page

If you create ads for multiple Facebook pages, select the Page you would like to create an ad for.

Choose your audience

In the ad targeting section, fill out the details of your audience. You can choose audience characteristics such as age, gender, interests and more. Learn about the targeting options available.

Critical Point Marketing

Select your ad placements

Decide where your ads will appear on Facebook, Instagram or Audience Network. If you select **automatic placements**, your ads will be shown to your audience in a place that it's likely to perform best. If you would like to do this manually, select **Edit Placements**. Learn more about selecting ad placements.

Placements
Show your ads to the right people in the right places.

- **Automatic Placements (Recommended)**
  Your ads will automatically be shown to your audience in the places they're likely to perform best. For this objective, placements may include Facebook and Instagram. Learn more.

  Edit Placements
  Removing placements may reduce the number of people you reach and may make it less likely that you'll meet your goals. Learn more.

Set your budget and ad schedule

In the budget & scheduling section, you can choose a budget and set your ad's schedule. Learn more about budget, delivery, and charges on your Facebook ads.

Critical Point Marketing

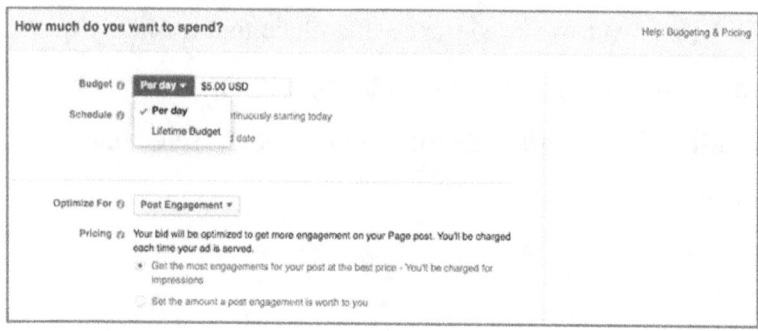

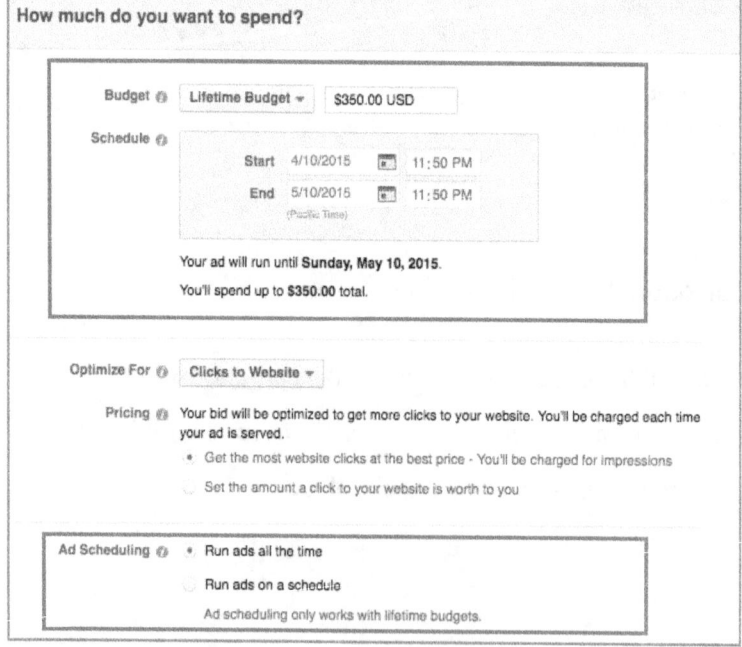

Learn about minimum daily budgets and how spending money on advertising works.

Set your bid

If you choose, you can set a manual bid by updating the **Optimize for** and **Pricing** sections with your preferences. Learn more about setting your ad's bid.

Naming your ad set

Next to **Ad Set Name**, add a name for your ad set or use the default name that appears.

Critical Point Marketing

Creating your ads

Select an ad format

Choose from several ad formats at this step: Carousel, single image, single video, slideshow, or Canvas.

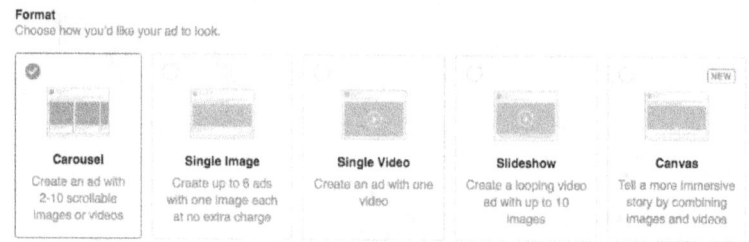

Choose your images

- Learn more about choosing images for your ad
- Check out design tips for Facebook ads
- Learn how to advertise successfully within Facebook's policies

Add text to your ads

After choosing your images, you can enter the text you'd like your ad to have.

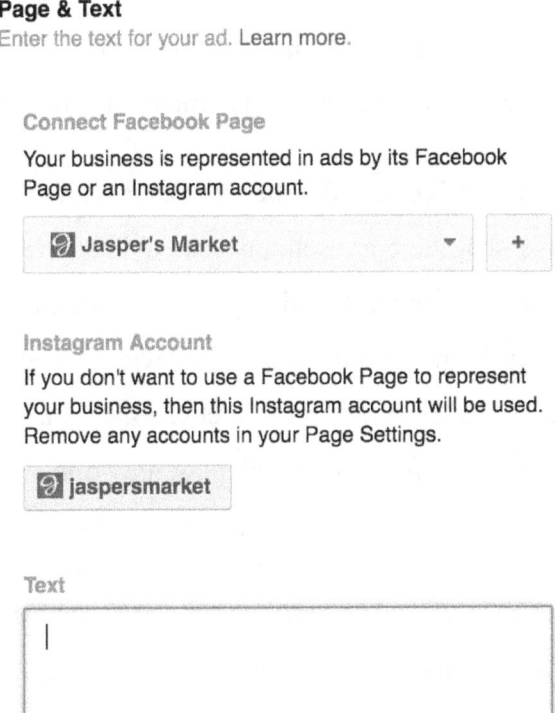

Note: If you're running ads that aren't associated with a Facebook Page, you'll only be able to run ads in the right column of Facebook.

Placing your order and choosing how you want to pay for your ads

When you're ready, click **Place Order** at the bottom of ad creation to order your Facebook ads. The first time you place an order, you'll be asked to enter your payment information.

Through the years we've found, when working with various social media ads, that there are some tweaks to keep in mind. First, the right side column ads tend to get less clicks and they don't show up in the newsfeed on mobile devices. Since the majority of Facebook users use mobile devices, it is a better use of your money to focus only on newsfeed ads, which everyone can see no matter what device they are using.

As with Google paid ads, it's beneficial to create two or three versions of your ad to see which ad has the higher click through rate and creates the best start for lead conversions. Multiple landing pages can also be created to test which pages convert to sales better than others. When you find an ad with a high click through rate and leads to better conversions, then you have a campaign worth funding with more and more of your marketing dollars, as long as you are achieving the ROI you need.

Social Media Summary

Critical point marketing means reaching your clients at critical points during the buying process. Many times, this critical point is the point before the potential customer has even thought about purchasing your product or service.

As in the case of a carpet cleaning company, perhaps the potential customer has realized the need to clean their carpets, but then forgot about this need, or let it slip their mind. If, however, you were to use a social media ad to show before and after photos of a newly cleaned carpet and offer a carpet cleaning special, then perhaps that would spur them into action. It's also not too farfetched to consider a potential client has not even thought about getting their carpets clean, and yet, once they see your ad, the idea is planted and you may end up with a customer you wouldn't have gotten otherwise.

Social media marketing is a great way to reach a targeted group of people who will most likely be the best candidates to purchase a product or service from you. Once you target that audience, you can then start to work on creating an emotional bond between your business and your potential customers while also advertising specials and offers to them.

Your main objective for marketing through social media is to help potential customers become familiar with you and your business, keeping in mind that these potential customers may not do business with you for a year or more. If you continue to use social media to build your brand or company awareness, it will pay off in the long run. The more people who know about you and recognize you, the better it is for your business no matter how these customer find you down the road.

Chapter 7: Content Marketing

"Content marketing is a strategic marketing approach focused on creating and distributing valuable, relevant, and consistent content to attract and retain a clearly-defined audience — and, ultimately, to drive profitable customer action".

-Content Marketing Institute

The main concept behind content marketing is that the word "content" refers to content that you create and own. Most marketing platforms are considered rented space. In other words, when you place your ads in other magazines, you're essentially renting that space. If you create the magazine, then the content is yours and you can advertise in your own content without renting the ad space.

There are plenty of examples of rented space but in the end, for most advertising mediums, any advertising you do is targeting someone else's audience and using their platform. In the world of SEO, content marketing means creating your own content to advertise with and building your own audience. Below are some examples of content that you could create vs renting space.

Rented Space

- Newspaper Ad-------Rented Space on Newspaper
- Facebook Ad---------Rented Space on Facebook
- Google PPC Ad------Rented Space on Google
- Billboard Ad---------Rented Space on Billboards
- Magazine Ad---------Rented Space in Magazine

Owned Content

- Monthly magazine or newsletter
- Blog posts on your website
- Your own video posted on social channels
- PowerPoints or other presentations
- Downloadable PDF
- Audio recording (podcast)

When creating any type of content, there shouldn't be page after page of "specials" like a coupon book, a video

or audio file with an extended sales pitch. Yes, you do want to advertise and promote your services in your content but it's best, as mentioned before, to follow the "4-1-1 Rule" – that is, for every 4 pages of high quality, and engaging content, you can have 1 page with a "Soft Push" and 1 page with a "Hard Push".

Food & Family Example

One of my favorite examples of how a company can take advantage of creating their own content is KRAFT Foods' magazine "Food & Family Magazine". This magazine offers a variety of stories and recipes. Since KRAFT is the creator of this magazine, the articles contain offers and advertisements for KRAFT food items. The magazine sells for only a few dollars, but how you would like it if your customers paid you to advertise to them. Therein lies the genius of this content marketing plan.

SEO & Content Marketing

When you create content full of information about the services you offer and you have links back to that content from other places like social media sites and press releases, you build good page authority and page relevance. This improves your SEO rankings on Google. As you create content, you want to ensure that the content is optimized with the keyword phrases you want to be ranked for (e.g., "carpet cleaning Logan, UT" or "upholstery cleaning Nashville, TN"). As people share your information and as you add more information about your specific services to your website, positive SEO rankings will follow.

Planning Your Content Marketing Campaign

When you are planning your content marketing campaign, think about how all the pieces will fit together.

- What is your content going to be about?
- How are you going to promote it?
- What social media accounts will you use and why?
- What are your social media posts going to say?
- What is the goal for your content marketing campaign?

As you prepare your content marketing strategy, remember to think about your content marketing from the perspective of the person you are targeting. Ideally, you want your content to be inviting, educational, inspiring, and touching to people on an emotional level. The more valuable and relevant your content is, the more people are going to want to share it. Keep in mind how you will use all of the different elements to promote your content and how you can encourage others to share it.

Content Marketing Summary

The objective behind a good content marketing campaign is to create content that is interesting, informative and attracts people to your site, while also giving you the ability to advertise and promote your services. When you create good content people will share it and come to your site regularly to get more ideas or be entertained. It's OK to advertise your specials and sell your services, but follow the "4-1-1 Rule" and only add one section each of "soft push" and "hard push" out of six total sections. As you plan your content marketing campaign, consider all the different ways you can promote it and create a plan that covers each element and also works with every other element so everything you do is integrated and has a purpose.

Critical Point Marketing

Chapter 8: Video Marketing

We live in a time when video is easily created and is very accessible. In years past, it would take thousands of dollars to create a good quality video commercial. Cameras were much more expensive, then there was the time it took to edit the video. If you wanted an aerial shot you hired a helicopter and again, paid thousands. These days you can record, edit and publish a video on a mobile device, and you can purchase a drone to record aerial footage for a few hundred dollars and use it over and over again.

Because video is becoming something so easy to create and publish there are millions of videos published every day. Rather than becoming less and less popular because of this, video is becoming more and more desired by the public. This sensation has created thousands of full time jobs on YouTube and in some cases ordinary folks can literally become millionaires almost overnight. In fact, according to statisticbrain.com, the latest YouTube numbers show that:

Critical Point Marketing

Total number of people who use YouTube	1,325,000,000
Hours of video uploaded to YouTube every minute	300 hours
Number of videos viewed on YouTube everyday	4,950,000,000
Number of unique visits to YouTube every month	900,000,000
Total number of hours of video watched on YouTube each month	3.25 billion hours
Number of YouTube videos that have generated over 1 billion views	10,113
Percent of YouTube visitors that come from outside the U.S.	70 %
Number of countries with localized versions of YouTube	42
Total number of languages Youtube is broadcast in	54
User submitted video with the most views – "Charlie bit my finger"	829,000,000
Average number of mobile YouTube video views per day	1,000,000,000
Average time spent on YouTube per mobile session	40 minutes
Average YouTube partner channel payout per 5,000 views	$0.32

One of the incredible features of YouTube is that you, or any individual can very easily create their own YouTube channel. According to Quora, the cost to start and maintain a cable television station is going to be in the hundreds of thousands of dollars annually. The cost to create a channel on YouTube $0. That must be because more people watch cable TV than YouTube.

In a recent study, we discovered that the average time a person spends on YouTube each day is about 30% more than the time spent watching cable television. For younger viewers, YouTube and other streaming networks are watched 2.5 times longer than standard Television.

These numbers speak volumes when it comes to understanding the power of video marketing. You don't have to have a million subscribers or followers in order to have a video viewed a few thousand times. In fact, just like PPC for the display network and social media, you can pay YouTube, owned by Google, to show your video to a specific type of target audience in a specific area.

Just as it is in social media and content marketing, the most enticing videos are those which cause an emotional response. The beauty of video is that video is one of the more powerful mediums to help people feel emotion. If you create a video that causes others to feel good, happy, or to laugh or even cry, that video will most likely be shared and viewed multiple times. This is especially true if you are willing to pay for views.

One recent video dubbed as "Chewbacca Mom" exploded into Facebook history by becoming the fastest growing viral video in 2016, and to date the video has been viewed over 165 million times. This video made such a big splash for a few reasons, but according to some experts the video offered a much needed relief from some of the pressures of 2016. According to one Hollywood reporter, Peter Mayhew, who has played Chewbacca said simply: "Absolutely wonderful! Cheers."

According to The Washington Post:

> "There's no exact science to what makes one video go viral online among the millions posted to social media every day.

But studies have shown the content that makes people feel good is what is most clicked and most shared.

Human emotion is contagious. Hearing another person's laughter triggers the part of the brain that controls smiling, according to scientific research. It's why sitcoms use laugh tracks. It's why watching Payne giggle from beneath the mask made us laugh, or at least smile, too.

But it's more than that. Payne's video is a reminder that life is filled with simple pleasures. Even with all the negativity in the world, you can drive to Kohl's, buy a toy for under $20 and crack yourself up alone in your car. It's uncomplicated. It's not stressful."

Once this video had gone viral, the Chewbacca mask displayed in the video sold out in all of the Kohl's around the country. This was not the intent of the video, but it demonstrates how an emotional connection can lead to huge sales numbers for a given product or service.

Video Marketing PPV

As mentioned earlier it is possible to pay to have your video viewed. Not everyone is fortunate to have the right kind of timing and video as Candace Payne (Chewbacca Mom), so you may want to invest a little to get your video in front of your target audience.

According to Google, here are the steps for creating a video ad campaign through Google Adwords:

Sign in to your **AdWords account**.

Click the **Campaigns tab**.

Note: Your video campaigns are located with your other campaign types (if any) from the "All campaigns" drop-down menu. You can also use this drop-down menu to view only your video campaigns by selecting Video campaigns.

Click **+CAMPAIGN**, and then click **Video**.

1. Enter a campaign name.
2. Choose a campaign subtype:
    a. "Mobile app installs"
    b. "Shopping".
3. For "Standard" campaigns, do the following:
4. Next to "Video ad formats" select **In-stream or video discovery ads**.
5. Enter a budget.
6. Choose the networks you want the video campaign to run on.
7. Choose the locations where you want to target (or exclude) your campaign.
8. Choose the language of your customers.
9. (Optional) Choose the devices you want to show your ads on. You can target particular operating systems, device models, and carriers. By default, your ads will show on all eligible devices.
10. (Optional) Edit your campaign's advanced settings.
11. Click Save and continue.
12. Enter an ad group name.
13. Next to "Your YouTube video," choose a YouTube video.

14. Next to "Video ad format" choose either **In-stream ad** or **Video discovery ad**. Enter the required information.
15. Set a bid amount.
16. Edit the targeting methods you want to use for your ads. By default, your ads will show to all viewers.
17. Click **Save ad group**.

As in a search or display network campaign, you will want to make sure that you check and double check your target audience and set a daily budget so you don't end up breaking the bank.

Video Marketing Summary

Video Marketing is a great way to reach thousands of people in your target market and offers an inexpensive way to create something that can make an emotional connection with your potential customers. Video marketing may not be on the top of your marketing list, however, it is something that is worth considering once you have mastered some of the other marketing concepts we've discussed thus far.

Chapter 9: Email Marketing

Email Marketing is by far one of the most lucrative opportunities for any business, provided that the business has a good database of customers to market and sell to. For most businesses, existing customers cost far less to market and sell to than marketing and selling to new customers.

Email marketing is a great way to acquire revenue from existing clients, but not a great marketing system for a brand new business. Many businesses become so focused on acquiring new customers that they forget the fact that they could have a few thousand dollars or a few million dollars even in revenue that could be obtained with nothing more than a well-timed email to an existing database.

If you are a new business just getting off the ground, the number one concern is to acquire new customers, however, with the long-term in mind, it's critical to remember to gather the customer's contact information for future marketing and offers. Keep in mind that even if every email contact you get is only worth one dollar a year in future revenue, if you end up with a list of 50,000 subscribers that's an easy $50,000 you can add to your bottom line. If you are a business with millions of contacts, well, you get the point, it can add up.

Anthony Morrison, one of the internet's well respected sources on making money online, tells the story of a business he shut down without considering the possibility of emailing his previous clients with offers for products for which he could profit. In his story he talks about the amount of money he made selling car parts online, but shut the business down once it became so time consuming.

He states in one of his writings that he sent an email to a database of a little over 9,000 of his newsletter subscribers and earned commissions of over $11k. Of course, this amount is just over $1 per customer email he'd acquired for this particular product. The real lesson learned here was that as he went back to view his database of contacts for the once popular car parts store, he realized he had over 400,000 emails he could have sent an offer to. Again, he could send an email selling parts for another vendor without having to fulfill the order himself. He may have been able to send an email selling a downloadable eBook on car restoration. There were several ways he could monetize that email list. The moral of the story is though, that with a simple email, Anthony could have generated a potential $400,000 just by remembering to email that list.

Too often, and the list of current contacts your business has may be ripe for a good email list that could generate some major sales, all you need to do is ask.

Creating an Email List

There are several different ways to create an email list. Research indicates that one of the best ways for a new business to grow a list of contacts is to offer those contacts something for free. If the customer is in your store, you can offer them 10% off their purchase when they sign up for your monthly newsletters or sign up for an email coupon list.

If the customer is not sitting right in front of you, or if you are trying to grow an email list online, then the top enticements include a free informational eBook, or a free downloadable catalog. Many digital marketers have found it valuable to offer a free newsletter that promises and delivers great ideas relevant to their particular customers. If your online business sells quilting materials then your newsletter could offer free quilting patterns. If your business sells something more virtual like online games, your newsletter could offer winning strategies for the top games.

There are probably many ideas you can come up with on your own that would be a good reason for someone to give you their contact information and more importantly, permission to contact them. Once you have their permission to contact them, you will want to make sure you only contact them with either information you think they will find valuable, or more importantly information they have told you they would like to have.

It's also important that you only contact your email list on a schedule they've given you permission for. It's ok to send out a daily email if that is what your contact wants or monthly if that is what they have given permission for. If the contact has signed up for a monthly email for example, but you send them an email every week, those contacts will almost assuredly opt out of your newsletter system. In the same manner of speaking, if you promise daily specials and only send them weekly, you are still going to disappoint them. The bottom line is you want to meet the expectations you've set and that they have agreed to.

Email Creation

When creating the emails to send to your contact list, you want to make sure you are giving them first and foremost, the type of information they are looking for. An email filled with nothing but a large sales pitch is never going to do well unless that is the type of email they are requesting. Most emails should follow the same rule we've previously discussed, the 4-1-1 rule.

One of the main focuses of an email should be the design. A good email will look good, be easy to navigate, and be attractive to the reader. While some of your contacts will only see a text version of your email, most email clients and browsers support HTML emails that are visually enticing as well as offering good quality content.

There are several email and newsletter systems that offer the ability to create and send great looking emails to hundreds and thousands of people in your email list. These email systems also offer the ability to gather email addresses and names directly from your website and input them into your contact database. A good email system can make a big difference in the quality of the email you create.

Although there are several email systems available, they almost all work the same way. First, you create the email by choosing an email theme or choosing a custom email option. Then you build your email one section at a time. You can add images, links and more almost as though you are building a web page. Once you have created your email, you then choose which list of contacts to send the email to, and choose a time and date to send it. That's it. You've sent your first email which starts your email marketing campaign.

Autoresponders

Autoresponders are an integral part of an email marketing campaign. An autoresponder is simply an email that you've prewritten that will be sent to an individual when they either send you an email, or sign up for a newsletter or order a product or service. Most email systems like those mentioned above will have the ability for you to create automated response.

Auto-reply emails are very good for several reasons. For

example, when someone orders a product or service, it's nice for them to receive an email outlining the details of the service or product they've ordered, like shipping information, or preparations they need to make for the scheduled service. When someone orders a product or service from you, it can help put your customer's mind at ease knowing you received the order and took the time to outline the details mentioned.

Auto response emails are also very good to use when a potential customer signs up for a newsletter. Sending an email quickly after they sign up can help them identify your brand and newsletter with the form they just filled out. Think about what may happen if they sign up for a newsletter, but you don't send your first email for a month. It's possible they may not remember signing up for the newsletter, and therefore, may cancel the subscription before it really even started.

Another great reason to use an autoresponder is to make the delivery of requested information almost instantaneous. Once someone fills out your form requesting a digital download for example, and email sent at that moment with the information requested will help your business to appear responsive and customer service oriented.

Email marketing is a great way to monetize the existing clients you already have in your customer database. If you are a new business and don't have many contacts, giving something away in trade for contact information is a great way to grow a contact list. As you communicate with your contact list you will want to make sure you deliver valuable and interesting content to them. If the emails you send are consistently doing nothing more than asking for them to purchase your product for service, you may find your subscribers will unsubscribe and you will lose that advantage.

As potential customers contact you, you will want to make sure you send an email immediately following their request so they can identify your business with the requested information more easily. Autoresponders can send these prewritten emails for you. Most email marketing systems have the ability to create auto response emails very easily.

Chapter 10: Creating Landing Pages That Convert

As mentioned in a previous chapter, landing pages can be any page that a potential or existing customer "lands on" when they click a link. These links can be from other websites, your own website, from an ad you've placed online or in an email. These ads can be placed on many social media platforms as well as on many search engines. No matter what link a potential customer clicks on to get to your landing page, you will want to make sure the page they are linked to has a clear message so that your advertising campaign doesn't hit a proverbial dead end.

There is no way to make a landing page that will convert the visitor to a sale every time, especially since there are so many different types of landing pages. Landing pages could be designed to:

- Solicit a newsletter signup
- Sell auto insurance quotes
- Offer a chance to win a trip around the world

Since there is such a wide variety of landing pages to be created, the best we can do is to give you some ideas digital marketers have identified as basic components every good landing page should have.

Keep in mind, that as in most cases, when it comes to digital marketing, the landing page should have a purpose in your online marketing campaign. Just throwing up a page and hoping something happens is a good way to get a whole lot of nothing. Your landing page should be carefully thought out and fit into your digital marketing campaign exactly how it's designed to fit.

Your landing page should match the same colors, images, lingo and message as your ads and other information that may lead to that landing page. When someone lands you're your page, you don't want them to feel lost or ask themselves how they arrived at that page. The page should have the same look and feel as the rest of your campaign components.

When it comes to the basic characteristics of a good landing page, you want your landing page to contain:

- A Clear and Intriguing Headline
- A Persuasive Subheadline

- Good Quality Images That Deliver the Right Message
- Brief Description of Who You Are and What You Do
- A Clear and Concise Offer (What's in it for them.)
- How you can help avoid pain
- How you can make "it" pleasurable
- Testimonials
- Guarantee
- Clear and Concise Call to Action
- Fill out the form to get started.
- Please list your name and the email you would like this FREE PDF sent to.
- Call Now and Start Saving Today.
- Signup Now For 10% Off Your First Order
- Start My Free Trial

Clear and Intriguing Headline

The headline on your landing page is usually the first thing someone reads when they see your page. That headline needs to set the tone for the rest of the page and tell the potential customer why they are there. It should capture their attention and give them an overall view of the intent of your offer. This headline should **NOT** be something like "Sign up for our newsletter", but something like: "Learn How Your Dirty Carpet Could Be Killing You" or "Learn the Top 10 Secrets to Successful Advertising". This headline should explain why they want to take action. This is not the moment you tell them to take action.

A Persuasive Subheadline

The subheadline should support the headline, not detract from it or introduce a new topic. See the example below:

> *Learn the Top 10 Secrets to Successful Advertising.*
>
> *These 10 secrets have been used by the fastest growing companies for the past 5 years, and they work like magic.*

The subheadline gives you the chance to say just a few words quickly, which can support the initial statement. A subheadline should also set up the explanation of the offer that the landing page is intended for. Both the headline and subheading should be bold and easy to spot, but it shouldn't be too flashy that they don't match the rest of the page look and feel.

© Robert Ratliff 2017

Good Quality Images That Deliver the Right Message

Example by: shopify.com

You've probably heard the old adage, "a picture is worth a thousand words." If not, it just means you can see in a good picture what it may take you a thousand words to explain.

Pg. 113

The image on the landing page can and should deliver a message that is enticing to the visitor.

The quality of the image makes a big difference in regard to the look and feel of the page. A small image on a landing page full of words just doesn't do well. The words are important, but often a good image with a few words can deliver the message in a stronger way, and look like less of a chore to read.

A high quality image is a professional image. Taking a selfie and adding it to your landing page will not deliver the professional message you are trying to send. If your landing page offers a product, then you will want to make sure your product is also portrayed well in the photograph. Again, taking a picture of your product sitting on a desk with your cell phone is not the right kind of image in most cases.

Brief Description of Who You Are and What You Do

The landing page should really be focused on the action you are hoping the reader will take. A brief explanation means everything you want to tell the customer should be explained in just a few short paragraphs. See the example below:

© Robert Ratliff 2017

Example by: www.impactbnd.com

In this example, you can see there is enough room to explain the offer fairly effectively, and at the same time the call to action is front and center, making it easy for the subscriber to take the next step.

Another example, as seen below, is to explain the benefits in short, concise bits of information. Again though, the call to action and action form are easy to see.

Example by: WebDam.com

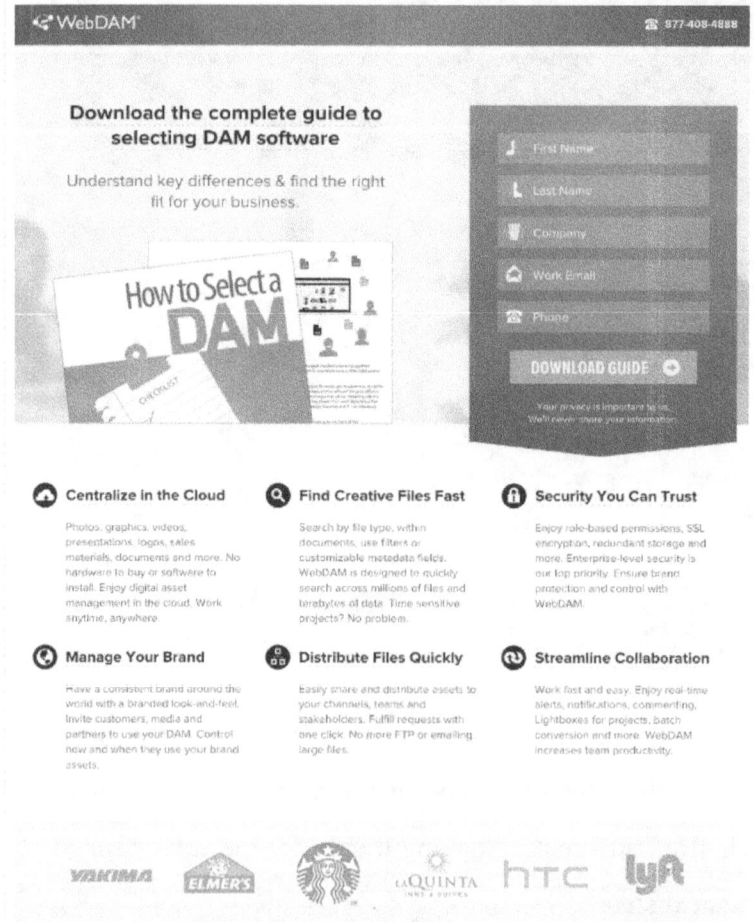

A Clear and Concise Offer (What's in it for them.)

You have someone looking at your landing page and they are thinking about whether or not they really want to give you their email and other contact information. Does your offer give them a good reason to give you their information? When you start to plan your campaign all of this information, including the offer, should be thought out so that the entire process is seamless. The ad headline and subheadline should match the headline and subheadline of the landing page. This helps the potential customer understand the offer better from the beginning, but also helps reduce costs for the ad.

If you remember in the chapter where we learned about PPC, we learned that if the ad matches the information on the page, you could get a higher quality score and therefore be given a lower cost per click for that ad. For this reason keeping everything in your campaign consistent is better for the reader, leads to better conversion, and could save you money in the long run.

When you write your offer, you really want to give the potential customer a reason to give you their information.

Critical Point Marketing

That reason may be to help them avoid pain or make their lives easier (offer a pleasurable outcome). It's important though, that as you write your offer, you keep it brief, but enticing. Below is an example of how three sentences can create an enticing offer.

Example by: Basecamp.com

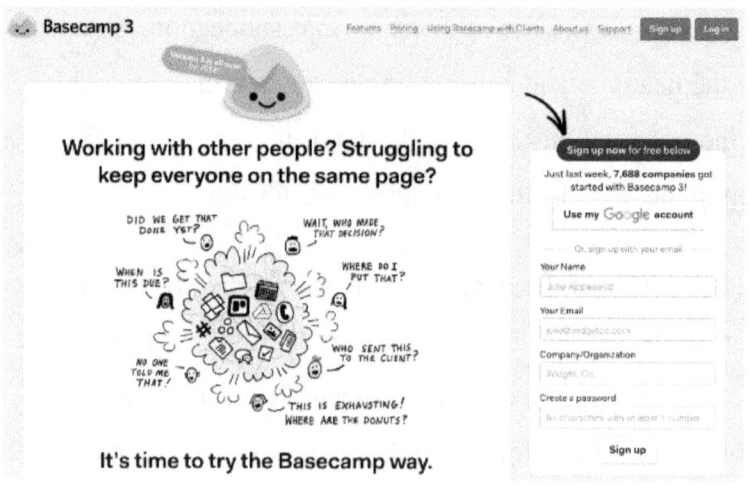

In the example above, there are three sentences: "Working with other people? Struggling to keep everyone on the same page? It's time to try the Basecamp way." These three sentences paint a pretty good picture about what Basecamp could do to help relieve some pain. The only thing I would have changed in this example would have been the sentence at the very bottom. It would be much more effective if it were something like: "Make life easier, try the Basecamp way today." This would submit to the reader that life can be easier and encourages the reader to take action today.

Testimonials

In the chapter where we first began learning about critical point marketing, I pointed out that 88% of consumers trust online reviews as much as a personal recommendation. This means that when you add testimonials from past customers/subscribers to your landing page, it's as good as having their friends or family tell them to sign in or join; well, 88% of the time. Adding testimonials is simply a must for that very reason.

Guarantee

When someone is looking to give you their information, or purchase a product or service from you, they may be hesitant to do so if they aren't familiar with your business. For this reason, a guarantee can help overcome that obstacle. The guarantee can be as simple as letting them know that if they aren't happy they can receive a complete refund. If a customer is subscribing to a newsletter, the guarantee could say something like "unsubscribe at any time" or that you won't sell their contact information to other companies.

Sometimes, especially if it's an eBook or low cost product, the posted guarantee will get them over the buyer's barrier, but when it really comes down to it they won't worry about the $6 dollars they spent enough to pursue a refund. Of course if they do want a refund it would be prudent to give them one, so they don't write a bad review or stir up any trouble for you online.

Guarantees should be written in a way to put the customer at ease so they won't be so concerned about taking the action you've requested on the landing page. You want your guarantee to connect with your viewer in a way that gives them a good feeling about your business. Guarantees show your customers that you are confident in your product and indicate you want them to be happy with their purchase. Below is an example of a guarantee.

© Robert Ratliff 2017

An UNBEATABLE Guarantee: Try *How to Talk to Anybody* for a full 60-Days, 100% Risk-Free

Try the entire course. If you don't LOVE it, I insist that you get 100% of your money back. I'll even eat the credit-card processing fees.

It's simple: Join the program and try it for yourself. If the powerful mental frameworks, strategies and scripts don't help improve your life in 60 days, I want you to email me. Show me you did the exercises, and I'll give you all your money back.

This guarantee lasts 60 days, which completely covers the course. That means you can try the ENTIRE course and then decide if it's right for you.

Clear and Concise Call to Action

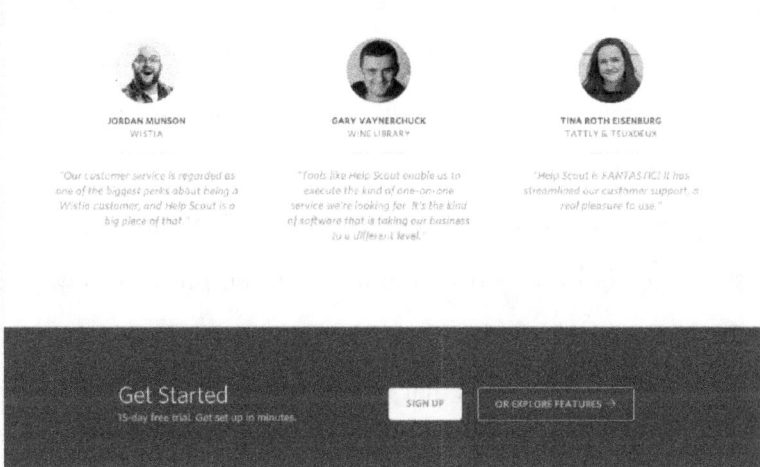

Pg. 121

Your call to action is one of the most important things to think about on your landing page. The call to action can sometimes be on the submit button. Rather than using the word "submit" on the submit button, you could use the words "Start Saving Now" or "Increase Profits Starting Today". Whatever it is that you decide to write as your call to action, you want to make sure it stands out. The best way to do this is to create a button that has a contrasting color to the other colors on your page. Below is an example of a call to action button that stands out.

Setting up Future Sales Using Your landing Page

On this landing page, you will also want to keep in mind that you can set the stage for future sales. If your business offers other products or services that work well with the specific product you're marketing, the landing page is a good place to mention these other products and how they can help support the main product or service you are selling. This way when the customer calls in to book a job or order the product they won't be caught by surprise that there are upgrades to the product or additional services that would benefit them.

Landing Page Summary

Your landing page is one of the last steps when it comes to your marketing campaign and also one of the most critical. A good landing page can make the difference between a future customer and just a page visit.

Landing pages should be well thought out, give the customer a reason to take action, look great, offer testimonials and guarantees, and most importantly, tell the potential customer exactly what they need to do. Your landing page copy should also be consistent with your email marketing, PPC ads or other pages, which link to your landing page. If you want to create a different type of offer, you need to go back to the drawing board and start developing a new campaign from the ground up. Don't just use an existing landing page if it isn't in line with a new ad campaign message.

Critical Point Marketing

Chapter 11: Measuring ROI

When it comes to marketing campaigns, you're always going to want to measure the results to either learn from mistakes, or to take advantage and repeat wins. Measuring ROI can mean so many different things depending mostly upon what your intentions were when you launched the campaign.

If your campaign was designed to increase sales, then you would want to measure the number of sales generated by the campaign. In most cases, you can use Google Analytics ecommerce tracking to measure the number of sales compared to the number of clicks that generated those sales. To enable ecommerce in your reports follow these steps:

If you need to enable Ecommerce reporting in the view in which you want to see the data. Here are the steps.

1. Sign in to your Analytics account.
2. Navigate to the desired account, property and view.
3. In the VIEW column, select Ecommerce Settings.
4. Click the Enable Ecommerce toggle ON.
5. Optional: Click the Enable Related Products toggle ON.

6. Click Next step.
7. Click Submit.

Google goes on to further explain:

Tracking setup with Google Tag Manager

If you use Google Tag Manager to manage your tracking, read the Ecommerce Tracking tag setup guide.

Tracking setup (web)

If you have not already added basic page tracking, do this first.

If you use a third-party shopping cart, or track transactions across separate domains, you'll need to set up cross domain tracking. If your shopping cart software is on the same domain as your ecommerce site, you don't need to implement cross domain tracking.

To collect ecommerce data from a website, you'll need to add JavaScript to your site that sends Analytics the transaction and item data. Refer to the Analytics Ecommerce Tracking documentation on Google Developers. If you are using Enhanced Ecommerce, refer to the Enhanced Ecommerce documentation.

Tracking setup (app)

To collect ecommerce data from a mobile app, use one of the Analytics SDKs.

To collect ecommerce data from an Internet connected device (a point-of-sale device, for example, but not a website or mobile app), refer to Ecommerce Tracking or Enhanced Ecommerce Tracking in the Measurement Protocol developer guide."

The main reason for using Google's ecommerce tracking is that it allows you to add a value to specific actions like completed sale, or web form lead, click etc. In Google's words "Ecommerce tracking allows you to measure the number of transactions and revenue that your website generates. On a typical ecommerce site, once a user clicks the "purchase" button in the browser, the user's purchase information is sent to the web server, which carries out the transaction. If successful, the server redirects the user to a "Thank You" or receipt page with transaction details and a receipt of the purchase. You can use the analytics.js library to send the ecommerce data from the "Thank You" page to Google Analytics."

If you don't have Google analytics but you do have sales numbers, then the simplest way to track the ROI for your campaign would be to add the total earned in sales and subtract the cost of your ads including Google PPC, Email costs, printed material costs, social media ad costs, and any other amount you spent on advertising for that campaign to see if you made more than you spent, and by how much. If you spent $5,000 in total for your campaign, but your sales Generated $20,000 then you have a 4:1 ROI.

When it comes to measuring success of a campaign, especially if you are looking to improve campaign performance, it's important to tie sales into each lead category. For example, rather than just knowing you made a 4:1 ROI during your campaign, you may want to know which ad, or which platform generated the most sales.

There are several different tools to use for this purpose. Most of the major social media sites and Google have a way to add a tracking pixel to your website. The tracking pixel is usually installed on the page that the customer sees once the sale is complete. This pixel sends a message to the referring site so that when you look at your Google or Facebook analytics report you can see how many completed sales you have compared to the amount of clicks.

This system also allows you to measure how many sales came from Facebook, vs Google, vs another advertising tool. In the case of Google, Facebook, and other major online advertising networks, their systems will track the purchaser from the click on the ad through the sales process. This way you can determine right down to the keyword what part of the campaign and which marketing sources lead to the most sales. You may find that Google paid ads were most helpful in generating sales, or you may find that with Facebook or Twitter.

In order to add a tracking pixel to a page from Facebook, you will follow these steps:

Creating a Facebook pixel for tracking

To create your Facebook pixel:

1. Go to your **Facebook Pixel** tab in Ads Manager.

2. Click **Create a Pixel**.
3. Enter a name for your pixel. You can have only one pixel per ad account, so choose a name that represents your business.

   Note: You can change the name of the pixel later from the **Facebook Pixel** tab.

4. Check the box to accept the terms.
5. Click **Create Pixel**.

Important: If you've created a Custom Audience pixel in the past, you have an older version of the Facebook pixel and won't see an option to create another. However, we strongly recommend that you update to the Facebook pixel base code and add its event codes to access all the products that can help your business.

About the Facebook pixel code

The Facebook pixel code is made up of two main elements:

- Pixel base code
- Event code

The pixel base code tracks activity on your website, providing a baseline for measuring specific events. The base code should be installed on every page of your website.

To install the pixel base code:

1. Go to the Pixels page in Ads Manger
2. Click **Actions** > **View Code**
3. Copy the base code and paste it between the <head> tags on each web page, or in your website template to install it on your entire website

Events are actions that happen on your website, either as a result of Facebook ads (paid) or organic reach (unpaid). The event code lets you track those actions and leverage them in advertising.

There are two types of events you can send:

- **Standard events.** 9 events we're able to track and optimize your ads for without any additional actions. See below for an example of what your website code will look like with standard events installed.

Critical Point Marketing

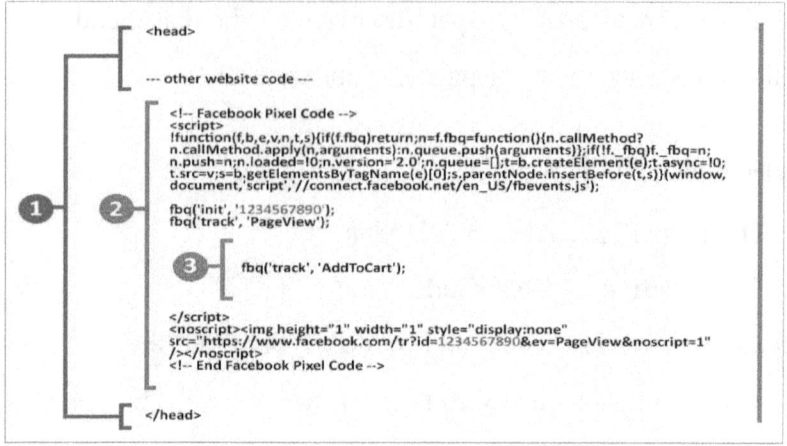

The Facebook pixel code with a standard event.

1. Your website's original code: Paste the Facebook pixel code between the **<head>** and **</head>** tags of your web page. You may already have other existing code between the head tags, so just place the pixel code underneath that, but above **</head>**.

2. Your Facebook pixel base code: Your Facebook pixel code will look like the diagram above, except your pixel ID will be different from 1234567890.

3. Your standard event code: Within your Facebook pixel code, above the **</script>** tag, paste the Standard Event code that's relevant to your page (ex: Complete Registration, Add

To Cart). You'll need to do this for every page you want to track.

The key here is that every page of your website should have everything that's enclosed in section 2 (the base code), but different pages will have different snippets of code for section 3 (standard event code). See below for another example.

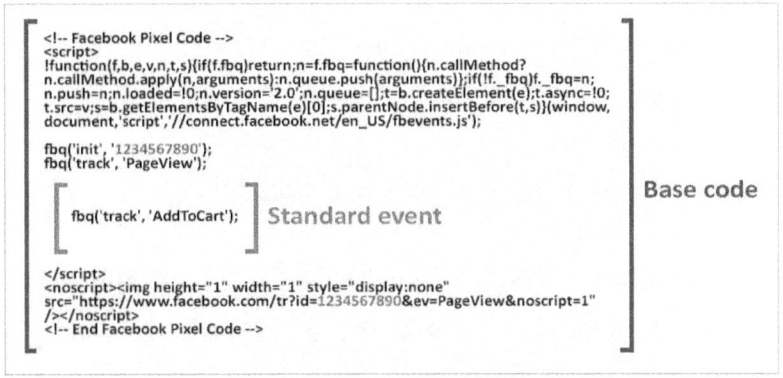

What the code looks like on an add-to-cart page.

- **Custom events.** Actions that are important to your business, but that you can't use for tracking and optimization without additional action.

Adding the Facebook pixel base code to your website's pages

To add the pixel code to your website:

1. Go to your **Facebook Pixel** tab in Ads Manager
2. Click **Actions** > **View Pixel Code**
3. Click the code to highlight it
4. Right-click and select **Copy** or use Ctrl+C/Cmd+C
5. Click **Done**
6. Go to your website's HTML and paste the code

Tip: We recommend that you put the code in the header tags of the website HTML to ensure that the it's able to track across your entire site.

Adding the event code to your website's pages

Event code indicates specific actions that are important to your business objective. To add the event code to your website:

1. Go to your Facebook Pixel tab in Ads Manager.
2. Click **Create Conversion** > **Track Conversions with Standard Events**.
3. Copy the Event Code of the events that matter to you.
4. Go to your website's code and place the event code on the relevant pages. We recommend doing this

by adding the event code between script tags separately. We recommend not modifying the pixel base code.

Tips: Add a full funnel of events (ex: ViewContent, AddToCart and Purchase) to capture all relevant purchase actions.

On the special pages of your website that you want to track and optimize your ads for, add one of these 9 standard events. For example, someone selling toys on their website would place standard event codes for their add-to-cart page and purchase page. Just copy and paste everything in the standard event code column and add it to the page on your website where you'd like to track this action. Be sure to avoid adding your standard event code to the header section of your website (where you add the Facebook pixel base code). If you do, you won't know on which page of your website a certain event happened. If you'd prefer to use URL rules instead of standard events, you can use custom conversions instead.

Critical Point Marketing

Website action	Standard event code
View content	fbq('track', 'ViewContent');
Search	fbq('track', 'Search');
Add to cart	fbq('track', 'AddToCart');
Add to wishlist	fbq('track', 'AddToWishlist');
Initiate checkout	fbq('track', 'InitiateCheckout');
Add payment info	fbq('track', 'AddPaymentInfo');
Make purchase	fbq('track', 'Purchase', {value: '0.00', currency: 'USD'});
Lead	fbq('track', 'Lead');
Complete registration	fbq('track', 'CompleteRegistration');

© Robert Ratliff 2017

Note: You can also add different parameters for each standard event code, such as Content ID, value and currency. The conversion standard event requires value and currency parameters to work. Parameters are optional for all other standard events.

I want to install just the image tag of the Facebook pixel

In some cases it may be necessary to use only the image tag of the Facebook pixel, such as when you're piggybacking off of existing container tags (ex: DFA, Atlas). In these scenarios, you should use the PageView image tag on every page of your site, then create another image tag for the standard events on specific pages.

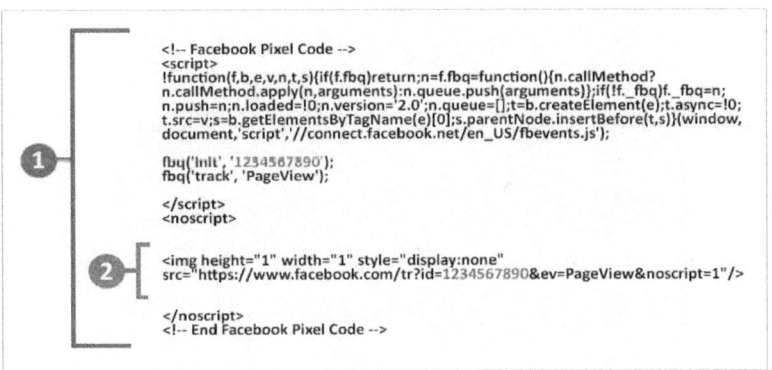

Pg. 137

1: The Facebook pixel code: We recommend using this entire code.

2: The image tag: Please make sure you don't copy the **<noscript>** tag as well.

Below is an example of how you'd set up Facebook pixel image tags across key pages of your website with just the image tag. Keep in mind you have to replace 1234567890 with your Facebook pixel ID, and adjust your parameters (ex: currency) depending on your website.

On a product page, you would have these two tags:

<img height="1" width="1" style="display:none" src="https://www.facebook.com/tr?id=1234567890&ev=PageView"/>

<img height="1" width="1" style="display:none" src="https://www.facebook.com/tr?id=1234567890&ev=ViewContent"/>

On your add-to-cart page, you would have these two tags (plus parameters for the AddToCart event):

<img height="1" width="1" style="display:none"

src="https://www.facebook.com/tr?id=1234567890&ev=PageView"/>

<img height="1" width="1" style="display:none" src="https://www.facebook.com/tr?id=1234567890&ev=AddToCart&cd[currency]=USD&cd[value]=0.00"/>

On your purchase page, you would have these two tags (plus parameters for the purchase event):

<img height="1" width="1" style="display:none" src="https://www.facebook.com/tr?id=1234567890&ev=PageView"/>

<img height="1" width="1" style="display:none" src="https://www.facebook.com/tr?id=1234567890&ev=Purchase&cd[currency]=USD&cd[value]=0.00"/>

Confirm your pixel is implemented correctly

The Facebook Pixel Helper is a tool that helps you check whether your Facebook pixel is working properly.

After you've installed the Facebook pixel on your website, go to a web page the pixel was placed on. If it's working, the pixel will send information back to Facebook and you'll be able to see activity in the Facebook Pixel page in your Ads Manager. Your pixel's status will also be set to **Active**.

The main graph on the Facebook pixel page shows total pixel traffic over time (the default view for all data on the dashboard is the past 7 days, but you can adjust it using the dropdown on the top right).

At a glance, you can tell whether the data is roughly where you would expect it to be. Does it generally match your website analytics reporting? To check, compare the Total Traffic number in the upper right-hand side with the total number of website visits in the past 7 days (as reported in your website analytics).

Keep in mind data on this page refers to the total number of pixel fires, regardless of whether they were associated with an ad. This means the total number should roughly align with your overall website/page visit volume, not just attributed traffic from Facebook. It's normal that Facebook's numbers may be different from a third party's, but if there's a very large discrepancy (or you don't see any pixel traffic), something may be wrong.

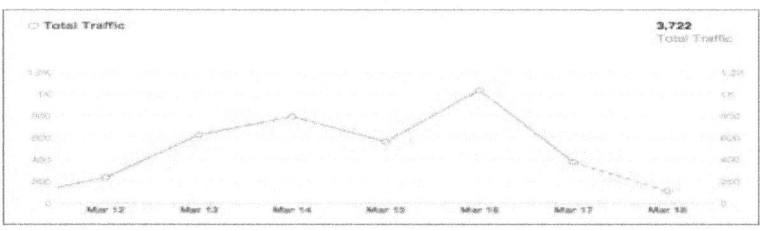

Check this graph to see your total pixel fires.

After you've checked your total pixel fires, you should ensure your events are being reported correctly. If you have events on any of your web pages, you should see them in your Events tab below your traffic graph. Both Standard and Custom Events will show up on this tab. If you have the wrong Event enabled, or it's set up on the wrong page, this will help you find it.

Events are case sensitive, so if you accidentally added **fbq('track', 'viewcontent');** to one of your web pages instead of the correct standard event code **fbq('track', 'ViewContent');** you'll see an event called **viewcontent** show up in the events tab instead (which will render as a custom event rather than a standard event), so you'll want to edit your pixel code on that page again to replace that code with the correct standard event code. Please note that PageView is the default event that the pixel fires on every page of your website (it's not a standard event).

Learn more about the other tabs available in this table.

Events	URLs	Domains	Devices		
Name		Status			Count (Last 7 days)
PageView		Active Last Received: 8 hours ago			1,452
ViewContent		Active Last Received: 8 hours ago			1,316
AddToCart		Active Last Received: 9 hours ago			61
Purchase		Active Last Received: 18 hours ago			15

Use the Events tab to troubleshoot your events.

Troubleshooting Pixel and Event Implementation

We recommend downloading the Facebook Pixel Helper to troubleshoot implementation problems. Keep in mind you have to be using the Chrome browser for it to work. Once the Pixel Helper is installed, a small icon will appear next to your address bar. Navigate to your website in your Chrome browser and click the Pixel Helper icon.

© Robert Ratliff 2017

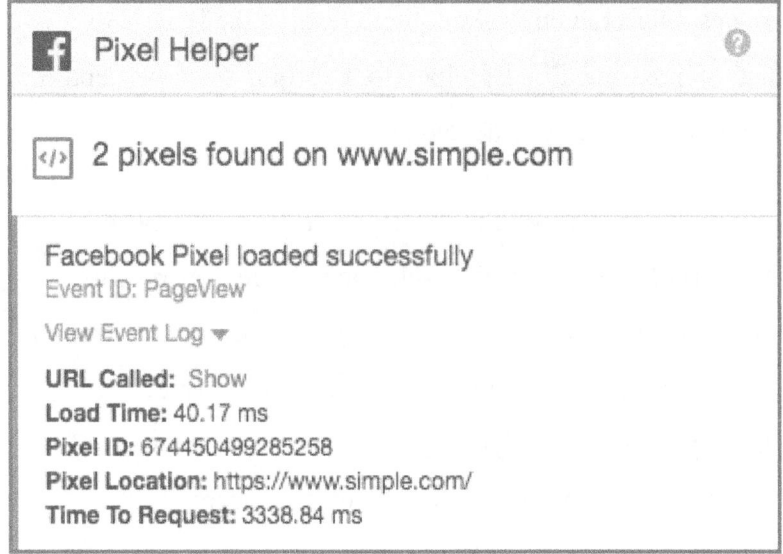

The pop-up will tell what pixels/events were found on the page, and whether they have loaded successfully. If you added standard events to your pixel code on certain pages, you'll need to complete a test conversion for each (ex. add an item to your cart to test an "AddToCart" event) in order to confirm that each event loads on the desired page or action. If your pixel's PageView event loads on every web page, and each of your standard events load successfully (on the desired pages only), you're ready to attach the Facebook pixel to your ads.

If the Pixel Helper tool displays errors or warnings on any of your pages, click **Learn More** to help resolve the issue. For a full list of possible Pixel Helper tool errors, warnings and recommendations, see our developers site.

In order to resolve most Pixel Helper errors you'll need to check the HTML code on the web page where you received the error. To check the HTML code, go to the desired web page and right-click on the screen, then select "Inspect" and search for your pixel ID (you can usually use "Control + F" or "Command + F" to bring up your browser's search bar).

- If you don't find the pixel ID anywhere in the code, it may have not been placed on that page. If you installed the pixel using a tag manager then you won't see the code on the actual web page, so you'll have to troubleshoot within your tag manager.
- If you do find the pixel ID, check the code carefully against your code in your pixel dashboard (under **Actions > View Pixel Code**) to make sure everything between the <script> and </script> tags is exactly the same and that the pixel wasn't placed in the middle of another code block

on your web page. You should find 2 instances of your pixel ID on each page where you placed the pixel (one in the <script> portion of the code and one in the <no script> portion. If you find more than 2, it's likely that the code has been placed multiple times, so you can delete any additional instances.
- When troubleshooting standard event implementation, make sure the the event code (ex. fbq('track', 'Purchase', {value: '0.00', currency:'USD'}); for a Purchase event) is placed either:
    1. Directly between the ";" after the PageView event and the </script> tag, or;
    2. Directly below the entire base code (in which case you'll need to add <script> directly before the event code and </script> directly after the event code).

Troubleshooting Custom Conversions

One of the most common issues with custom conversion rules

is when using the URL Equals option, as it will not count a conversion if someone lands on a version of the URL with any additional text beyond what is pasted into the URL field here (ex: UTM parameters, http vs. https, or even an extra "/" at the end).

To maximize your ability to track your custom conversion accurately, we suggest using URL Contains and pasting the minimum portion of the URL needed to distinguish this page from any other pages on your website (ex: Starting after "www" and ending before ".com", ".org").

Troubleshooting Ad Performance

One important thing to note in order track ad performance properly when using the Facebook pixel is that you'll need to customize your ads reporting columns in Ads Manager in order to show the most important data. By default, the Results column for a Website Conversions campaign will display the total number of events/conversions associated with your ads. That means if you have ViewContent, AddToCart and Purchase events on your website, the Results column will display the aggregate number of all these events, and the Cost column will display the cost per the total number of these events as well. If you really only care about the number of Purchases and cost per Purchase, you'll need to customize your columns to select "Purchase (Facebook Pixel)" and "Cost per Purchase (Facebook Pixel)."

If you've just transitioned from the old conversion pixel and are optimizing for conversions, you may experience a few days of decreased performance while the new pixel gathers the data needed to optimize sufficiently. Please review the Optimization section in the Conversion pixel transitioning guide for recommendations and best practices.

If you're optimizing for conversions and find that you're unable to spend your daily budget (due to under-delivery) and are seeing a high cost per conversion, there's a good chance your ads are not getting enough conversions to provide sufficient data to our delivery system in order to optimize (which needs about 25 conversions to start optimizing properly). If you set a target bid, you may also see delivery decrease if our system is unable to get conversions at the desired target bid. This is often due to having small or overlapping audiences, low bid to budget ratio, poor creative/targeting or high negative feedback

Defining conversions

In order to track and optimize for events on your website that matter to you, you need to define them as conversions. Standard events are already conversions, so if you're using standard events, there are no extra steps needed. They'll be available for you to track or optimize on.

If you're using custom events, plan to use URL-based rules, or want to define a conversion as a specific subset of standard events, you'll need to take the steps detailed below.

Using custom events as conversions

To use custom events as conversions:

1. Implement custom events in your page code
2. Go to your Facebook Pixel tab in Ads Manager
3. Click **Create Conversion > Track Custom Conversions**
4. In the "Rule" section, click the dropdown and change **URL Contains** to **Events**

    Note: It may take a moment for **Events** to appear

5. In the field underneath the dropdown, select the custom event you want to define as a conversion
6. In the "Category" section, click the **Choose a Category** dropdown and select the most appropriate choice
7. Name the custom conversion

You can also add a default conversion value, which we'll use if values aren't being sent dynamically as a parameter within the custom event. When a value isn't set or sent, we'll set it to 0 by default.

View your custom conversions.

Using a subset of standard events as conversions

To use a subset of standard events as conversions:

1. Go to your Facebook Pixel tab in Ads Manager.
2. Click **Create Conversion > Track Custom Conversions**
3. In the "Rule" section, click the dropdown and change **URL Contains** to **Events**.

   Note: It may take a moment for **Events** to appear.

4. In the field underneath the dropdown, select the

standard event.

5. If the event has sent parameters with it, you'll be able to select the key pair value. If you do not see it but expect it, make sure the event is set up to send data in parameters.
6. In the "Category" section click the **Choose a Category** dropdown and select the most appropriate choice
7. Name the custom conversion.

You may also add a default conversion value. We'll value the given conversion at the amount you specify if values aren't being sent dynamically as a parameter within the custom event. When a value isn't set or sent, we'll set it to 0 by default.

View your custom conversions.

Running your campaign

To create a campaign using your pixel:

1. Go to ad creation
2. Select the **Increase conversions on your website** objective
3. Click **Continue**

4. Choose a conversion event
5. Finish creating your campaign, making sure you:
    - Select **Conversions** as your "Optimization for Ad Delivery" choice at the ad set level
    - Enter the URL of the page you want to track conversions on in the "Destination URL" field at the ad level
6. Click **Place Order** when you're done

Keep in mind you can use the Facebook pixel in the same way when creating your ads in Power Editor. Your ad will automatically track all available conversion events so you don't need to manually select a pixel for tracking. You'll be able to see all this data in your ads reports.

https://www.facebook.com/business/help/952192354843755?helpref=faq_content#verify

By adding tracking pixels to post conversion pages, you will be able to track where those conversions came from and what keywords were used that led to the conversion. You can also track which pages were visited during the sales process to see if there is anything on those pages that could be altered for better results.

Call Tracking

Let's say that some of your sales aren't through a website, but that a customer calls in directly. In this case, you need a way to track the calls that come in and which source generated those calls. Enter call tracking.

The main reason to use call tracking is to determine which ad, coupon, billboard, or email generated the call. Call tracking software allows you to purchase several different phone numbers, but forward all those phone numbers to the sales queue. When someone calls that number, the software registers that in a call log. When you look at the call log, you will see how many times each number was dialed and in some cases the call tracking software will record the calls to help with training your sales representatives.

Like tracking pixels, calls can also be linked back to the searches or keywords used to send potential customers to a certain phone number. These calls can also be used to trace which paid ads generated the most traffic and where the potential customer saw the ad.

If your business takes sales calls or accepts job bookings through phone calls, then call tracking is a must if you really want to see what drives your sales. Call tracking allows you to track calls from any place you add a phone number.

Call Tracking DNI

Call tracking can be set up in a way that will allow you to show a specific phone number on your website when a visitor is generated from one of your ads. This is possible using a javascript code called dynamic number insertion (DNI). Dynamic number insertion is a small script that looks for the phone number you have on your website currently, and changes the number in real time when a customer click to your website from another source. If for example a customer clicks to visit your site from Facebook, the phone number on your website will change to show the Facebook assigned call tracking number.

By using DNI, you can track leads from their source even if they visit your website before they call. When this is executed properly, you get a much better idea of what ads or lead sources are working better than others. If you didn't use the DNI you may be inclined to attribute all leads to natural rankings, or existing website traffic, rather than attribute the traffic back to the real lead source.

To activate the DNI ability, a small bit of code will need to be placed on your website, most likely in the header section of each page you would like the DNI action to take place. The code will go between the <head> and </head>. Where you place the code could be different on various websites, so it's best to contact your call tracking software company to ask them for sure.

Each call tracking software will have its own version of this code. The code should be easy to find no matter which call tracking software company you use. If you are not able to find this code, a simple call to your call tracking provider should work to resolve the issue.

Using tracking pixels and call tracking is a great way to track real actions like completed sales or newsletter sign ups, but if your campaign is designed to improve brand awareness or heart share, then you are going to need to some type of polling, whether it's through cold calling or survey, in order to track your campaign results.

Measuring Results Summary

No matter what you are advertising or what campaign you are running, you could literally be throwing money out the door if you aren't tracking your results properly. Whether you are polling people in your community, using online or call tracking, measuring the results of your campaigns and tracking the success of advertising sources is critical to a good marketing.

By using proper tracking techniques, you can eliminate money spent in places that do not produce growth and add funds to those places that do. With the proper types of tracking you can find which paid ads, website pages, and keywords generate the most sales. Any type of tracking data can help you increase profitability in a big way, so measure your results. It's important.

Critical Point Marketing

Chapter 12: Putting it all Together

The purpose of the previous chapters were intended to introduce you to the tools that will help you create a successful marketing campaign strategy. When you use the tools together effectively, you can generate a better return on investment, than if you were to use each tool individually.

Pay-per-click marketing is more effective when used in conjunction with social media marketing, email, and SEO. SEO is more effective when PPC, social media and email help potential customers recognize your business name. Social media marketing is more effective when used in conjunction with PPC and email; and the list goes on.

The example below illustrates the necessity of creating a marketing strategy involving the combined power of the tools explained throughout this book. I worked with a carpet cleaning company in a small town in Arkansas.

The first step to developing our digital marketing strategy was to determine a carpet cleaning special they could offer in the communities they serve. The special was "3 rooms for $119 plus a free hallway cleaning". Before I go into more detail, first I want to make it known that the average job income was closer to $260, which is a little more than double the offer. This income was in large part due to the ability of the carpet cleaning technician to upsell additional services and perks, like stain guard, pet urine removal and more.

This ability to capitalize on the leads generated by your marketing campaign is a great way to increase the rewards associated with a good first step. Also keep in mind any new customers you are able to win with your new marketing strategy can continue to add to your company's bottom line for years to come. Each new customer should be treated like gold because each customer offers monetary value to your business.

Once we decided on an offer to base our campaign on, we developed ads for social media platforms, Google Display Network, and Google Search Network. We also built the pages that the ads would link to on the website, then purchased tracking phone numbers so we could track which ads lead to which calls. Finally, we created the copy that would be used for emails, and articles we sent to the local chamber of commerce and the home builders association in the area we were targeting.

Here is a checklist of the media we created:

1. Ads for the Google display network
2. Ads for the Google search network
3. Landing page content for which the ads would link to
4. Ads for Facebook and Instagram
5. Articles which would be sent to the local chamber of commerce and the local home builders association of which they were members. These articles contained a link back to the landing page we created.
6. Email that would be sent to existing customers with links back to the landing page.

Once we finished creating this content, we added the page copy and created the landing pages. This way, any clicks from the various ads would be sent to the proper location. If we had created the ads first and launched the ads, we would not have a place to link the ads to. This is why we created the landing pages first.

Now that we have a place for the landing pages to link to, we then placed the ads we developed in the various ad systems.

The ads were placed on Facebook, Instagram, Google search network, and the Google display network.

For the ads displayed in the Google display network, we created image ads of various sizes with the call tracking phone numbers we purchased, that way if a potential customer wanted to contact us they could do so without clicking the ad, saving the customer time and us money. If the customer did click on the ad, they would have been linked to the landing page we created and the call tracking number on the image ad would have been a match to the phone number displayed on the landing page. Again, this is possible due to dynamic number insertion.

Versions of this same ad were placed on Facebook. The only difference in the ad was the phone number placed in the Facebook ad was the call tracking number linked to track only Facebook leads. This way we could track how many calls were generated from Facebook.

During the process of creating the image and search ads for Instagram, Facebook and Google, we added the retargeting code to the landing page we created. Remember, this is a small bit of code that is placed as a cookie on a visitor's browser, so that once they visited our landing page they would then see our ad again and again on many different websites.

Next, we created another article, similar to the newsletter articles that the client could send to her existing database. This email contained a call tracking number for "email" advertisements and a link to the landing page.

1. We created a landing page with a clear and enticing offer that also contained a clear call to action: "Call or Book Online Today!"
2. Ads were placed in such a manner to target women 35-55 who owned pets, a house and who were married or single.
3. The ads were placed in a geographic region close to where this carpet cleaning company operated.
4. The ads were created to be enticing with both its offer and visual display.
5. We sent emails to their existing database of clients with a link to view the special.
6. This landing page contained the code necessary to

retarget customers by showing them our ad on Facebook and other websites they visited.
7. Articles were sent to the home builders' association and the local chamber of commerce. The article was sent to hundreds of businesses and homes and contained a link back to the landing page we created.

With all of this in place, a few thousand of potential customers were within reach. These potential customers would either get an email, read an article or see an ad that would link to the carpet cleaning company's website. Once they visited the landing page to view the offer, they would then see the same ad for the same special across multiple websites, namely Facebook and Instagram.

With this marketing strategy, we have covered the critical points for marketing. These points are:

1. When the potential customer is actively seeking carpet cleaning. (This we did by placing ads in Google's search network.)
2. Before the customer thought about carpet cleaning.

(Display and Social Media Ads)

3. When the customer clicked that ad, we presented them with a landing page that was specifically designed to show a very enticing special with a specific call to action.
4. We continued to show them the ad, reinforcing the desire to take action in order to have a cleaner carpet for a reduced cost by saving them money.
5. Once the appointment was made, the technician was able to upsell additional items that were shown on the landing page like stain removal, pet urine removal, stain protection etc.

By using the above principles, we were able to market to a potential customer at the most critical points in the sales process and continue to market to those customers again and again over a specified amount of time.

When we used this campaign strategy, we saw a return on investment of around 9:1. According to the revenue generated, the month we ran this campaign was the best month they had in nine months. The client also confided in me that the year before, they spent about five times the amount we spent for this campaign to achieve about the same results.

While I can't be certain how the money was spent the year before, what I can tell you is that when you use all the tools discussed and outlined in this book in the manner in which I've laid it out for you, each marketing tool can work synergistically with the others for a more profitable gain. As you look to start your own marketing strategies, I encourage you to take advantage of all the tools available, even if it means you need to spend less for each one, than spend more on one particular marketing channel.

www.ingramcontent.com/pod-product-compliance
Lightning Source LLC
Chambersburg PA
CBHW070230180526
45158CB00001BA/320